Psalms
and
Prayers

Publications International, Ltd.

Scripture quotations from *The Holy Bible, King James Version*

Images from Shutterstock.com

Copyright © 2025 Publications International, Ltd. All rights reserved. This book may not be reproduced or quoted in whole or in part by any means whatsoever without written permission from:

Louis Weber, CEO
Publications International, Ltd.
8140 Lehigh Avenue
Morton Grove, IL 60053

Permission is never granted for commercial purposes.

ISBN: 978-1-63938-868-4

Manufactured in China.

8 7 6 5 4 3 2 1

Let's get social!
 @Publications_International
 @PublicationsInternational
www.pilbooks.com

Table of Contents

Introduction	4
Prayers for Every Day	6
Forgiveness and Mercy	48
Faith	86
Love	116
Comfort and Healing	160
Trust	206
Praise	252
Thanksgiving	318
God's Presence	356

Hear my prayer, O God; give ear to the words of my mouth.

Psalm 54:2

Thousands of years after they were written, the Psalms are a rich storehouse that still speak to us today with their bluntness and honesty. We can identify with the writers of the book of Psalms as they worship and praise God, grapple with grief and distress, and struggle with fears and conflict.

In **Psalms and Prayers**, quotes and passages from the Psalms are paired with prayers and reflections about daily life today. You'll also find other songs and prayers that have stood the test of time, from lyrics of favorite hymns to prayers and blessings drawn from the Bible and Christian tradition.

In the first chapter, "Prayers for Every Day," you'll find an assortment of beloved traditional prayers and Bible passages, as well as prayers for morning, evening, and meals. The other chapters of the book each have a specific focus, so you can find a prayer or song that fits your situation or mood as you pray.

Psalms and Prayers may give you words to use as you pray, or may inspire you to pray or sing with your own words, knowing that the Lord of all hears you as surely as he heard the writers of the book of Psalms.

PRAYERS FOR EVERY DAY

Prayer does not change God, but it changes him who prays.

—Søren Kierkegaard

The Lord is my shepherd; I shall not want.

He maketh me to lie down in green pastures: he leadeth me beside the still waters.

He restoreth my soul: he leadeth me in the paths of righteousness for his name's sake.

Yea, though I walk through the valley of the shadow of death, I will fear no evil: for thou art with me; thy rod and thy staff they comfort me.

Thou preparest a table before me in the presence of mine enemies: thou anointest my head with oil; my cup runneth over.

Surely goodness and mercy shall follow me all the days of my life: and I will dwell in the house of the Lord for ever.

—Psalm 23

> Pray without ceasing.
>
> —1 Thessalonians 5:17

> No one should give the answer that it is impossible for a man occupied with worldly cares to pray always. You can set up an altar to God in your mind by means of prayer. And so it is fitting to pray at your trade, on a journey, standing at a counter or sitting at your handicraft.
>
> —St. John Chrysostom

Sweet hour of prayer,
sweet hour of prayer,

That calls me from a world
of care

And bids me at my
Father's throne

Make all my wants and
wishes known!

In seasons of distress and grief,

My soul has often found relief,

And oft escaped the
tempter's snare

By thy return, sweet hour
of prayer.

—William Walford

After this manner therefore
pray ye:

Our Father which art in heaven,

Hallowed be thy name.

Thy kingdom come,

Thy will be done in earth,

as it is in heaven.

Give us this day our daily bread.

And forgive us our debts,

as we forgive our debtors.

And lead us not into temptation,

but deliver us from evil:

For thine is the kingdom, and
the power,

and the glory, for ever.

Amen.

—Matthew 6:9–13

Thomas answered and said unto him, My Lord and my God.

—John 20:28

Come, Thou Holy Spirit, come;
And from Thy celestial home
Shed a ray of light Divine:
Come, Thou Father of the poor,
Come, Thou source of all our store,
Come, within our bosoms shine:
Thou of Comforters the best,
Thou the soul's most welcome guest,
Sweet refreshment here below:
In our labour rest most sweet,
Grateful coolness in the heat,
Solace in the midst of woe.
O most Blessed Light Divine,
Shine within these hearts of Thine,
And our inmost being fill:
Where Thou art not, man hath nought,
Nothing good in deed or thought,
Nothing free from taint of ill.

—Whitsunday, *Book of Common Prayer,* Church of England

God give us grace to accept with serenity the things that cannot be changed, courage to change the things that should be changed, and wisdom to distinguish the one from the other.

—Reinhold Niebuhr

> Praise waiteth for thee, O God, in Sion: and unto thee shall the vow be performed. O thou that hearest prayer, unto thee shall all flesh come.
>
> —Psalm 65:1–2

You hear all prayers, Great God. Young or old, rich or poor, we can bring our praise, our needs, and our concerns to you. Thank you!

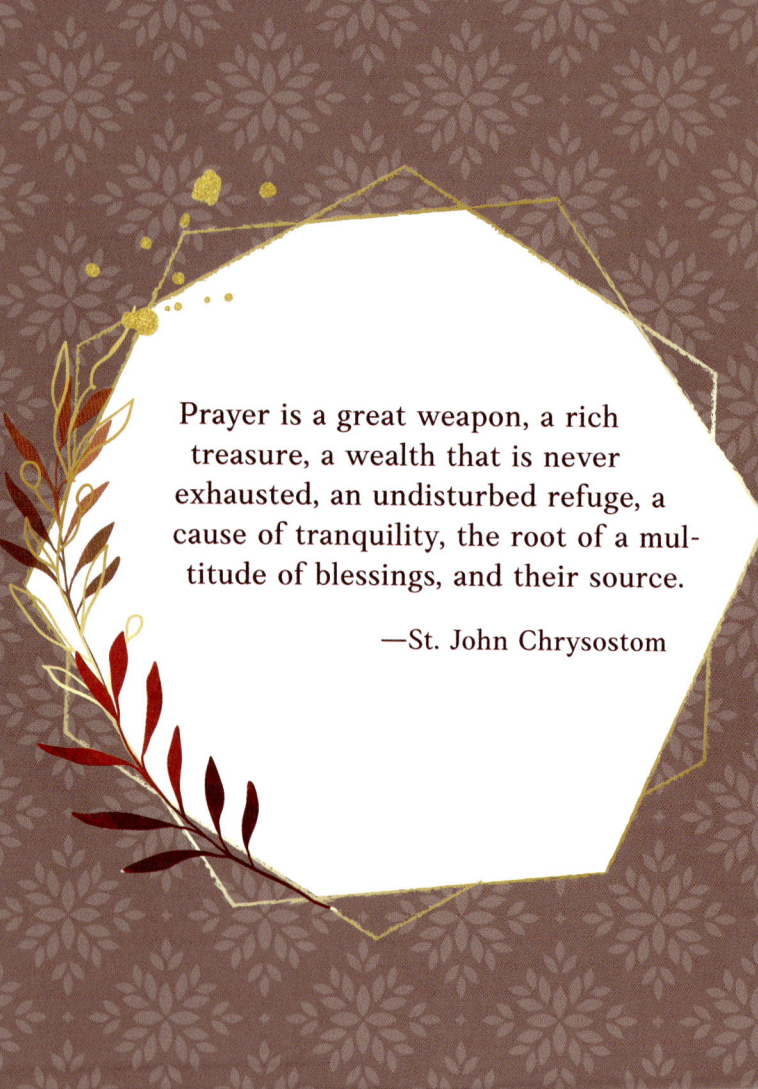

Prayer is a great weapon, a rich treasure, a wealth that is never exhausted, an undisturbed refuge, a cause of tranquility, the root of a multitude of blessings, and their source.

—St. John Chrysostom

Come and hear, all ye that fear God, and I will declare what he hath done for my soul. I cried unto him with my mouth, and he was extolled with my tongue. If I regard iniquity in my heart, the Lord will not hear me: But verily God hath heard me; he hath attended to the voice of my prayer. Blessed be God, which hath not turned away my prayer, nor his mercy from me.

—Psalm 66:16–20

Begin the morning with a song and a prayer, and the rest of the day will take care of itself.

> Give ear to my words, O Lord, consider my meditation. Hearken unto the voice of my cry, my King, and my God: for unto thee will I pray. My voice shalt thou hear in the morning, O Lord; in the morning will I direct my prayer unto thee, and will look up.
>
> —Psalm 5:1–3

Good morning, God! We greet you with our many morning faces. We arise sometimes grumpy, sometimes smiling, sometimes prepared, sometimes behind. Always may we turn to you first in our family prayer. Bless us today and join us in it.

The morning bright
With rosy light
Has waked me from my sleep;
Father, I own
Thy love alone
Thy little one doth keep.

All through the day,
I humbly pray,
Be thou my Guard and Guide;
My sins forgive
And let me live,
Blest Jesus, near thy side. Amen.

—Traditional prayer

Now I raise me up from sleep,

I thank the Lord who did me keep,

All through the night; and to him pray

That he may keep me through the day.

All which for Jesus' sake, I say. Amen.

—Traditional prayer

Cause me to hear thy lovingkindness in the morning; for in thee do I trust: cause me to know the way wherein I should walk; for I lift up my soul unto thee.

—Psalm 143:7–8

Coffee is part of the morning ritual at our house. Whoever gets up first gets the pot started; the familiar gurgling sound of the coffeemaker and rich smell of the coffee provide a comforting wake-up call. We plan the coming day "over coffee," and it is a meditative time of looking forward, of anticipation for all that is to come. What morning touchstones begin your day?

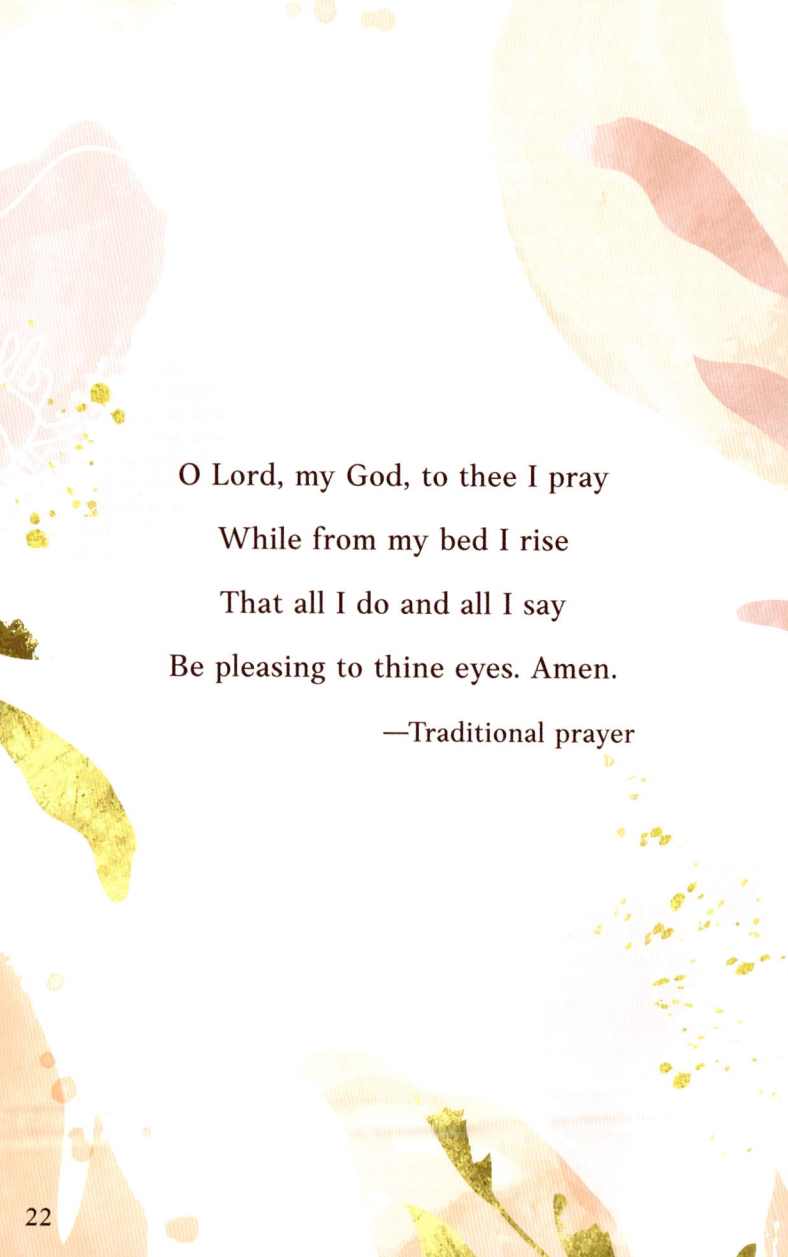

O Lord, my God, to thee I pray

While from my bed I rise

That all I do and all I say

Be pleasing to thine eyes. Amen.

—Traditional prayer

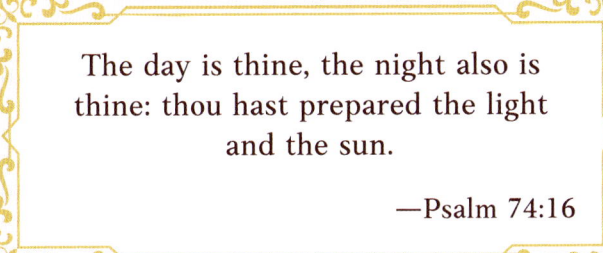

> The day is thine, the night also is thine: thou hast prepared the light and the sun.
>
> —Psalm 74:16

I can create the space to slow down and cherish the good things in life. Each day, I have at least one gift for which to be grateful: seeing the sun rise on a new morning.

In the early morning,
With the sun's first rays.
All God's little children
Thank and pray and praise.

I, too, thanks would offer,
Jesus, Shepherd dear,
For thy tender pasture,
For thy guiding care.

And I would implore thee,
Be with me this day,
Lest I from thee wander,
Into danger stray. Amen.

—Traditional prayer

> But I will sing of thy power;
> yea, I will sing aloud of thy mercy
> in the morning: for thou hast been
> my defence and refuge in the day of
> my trouble.
>
> —Psalm 59:16

As I send my family from our home this morning, Lord, I cannot be with each of them, so I trust them to your care. Please watch over them.

Put peace in my children's hearts. Protect them from harm, and grant them strength and courage to face each day. Make my husband equal to the mental and physical demands made upon him.

When their day of school or work is over, give them the satisfaction of having done their best and the assurance they will be welcomed home with loving arms.

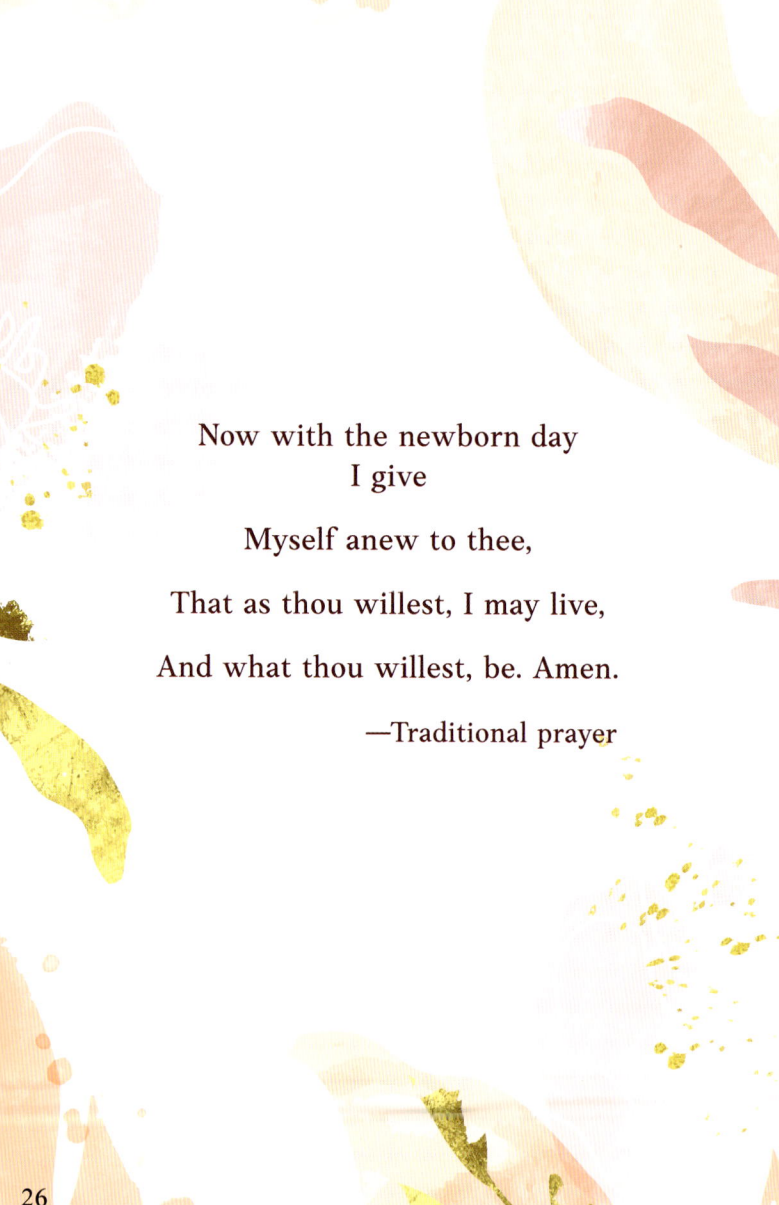

Now with the newborn day
I give

Myself anew to thee,

That as thou willest, I may live,

And what thou willest, be. Amen.

—Traditional prayer

> Lord, may I be wakeful at sunrise to begin a new day for you, cheerful at sunset for having done my work for you; thankful at moonrise and under starshine for the beauty of the universe. And may I add what little may be in me to your great world.
>
> —The Abbot of Greve

> Evening, and morning, and at noon, will I pray, and cry aloud: and he shall hear my voice.
>
> —Psalm 55:17

Sometimes, God, I pray to you in the morning, and turn my day over to you—and then I forget about you in the rush of the day. Please let me keep my thoughts fixed on you, so that I pray throughout the day, turning to you with my joys and sorrows.

May the babe of Bethlehem
be yours to tend;

May the Boy of Nazareth be
yours for friend;

May the Man of Galilee his
healing send;

May the Christ of Calvary
his courage lend;

May the Risen Lord his
presence send;

And his holy angels defend
you to the end.

—"Pilgrim's Prayer," found in
Oberammergau, Germany

He causeth the grass to grow for the cattle, and herb for the service of man: that he may bring forth food out of the earth.

—Psalm 104:14

Grant us thy grace, O Lord, that, whether we eat or drink, or whatsoever we do, we may do it all in thy name and to thy glory. Amen.

—Traditional blessing before meals

> For thou shalt eat the labour of thine hands: happy shalt thou be, and it shall be well with thee.
>
> —Psalm 128:2

> Great God, thou Giver of all good,
>
> Accept our praise and bless our food.
>
> Grace, health, and strength to us afford
>
> Through Jesus Christ, our blessed Lord.
>
> Amen.
>
> —Traditional blessing before meals

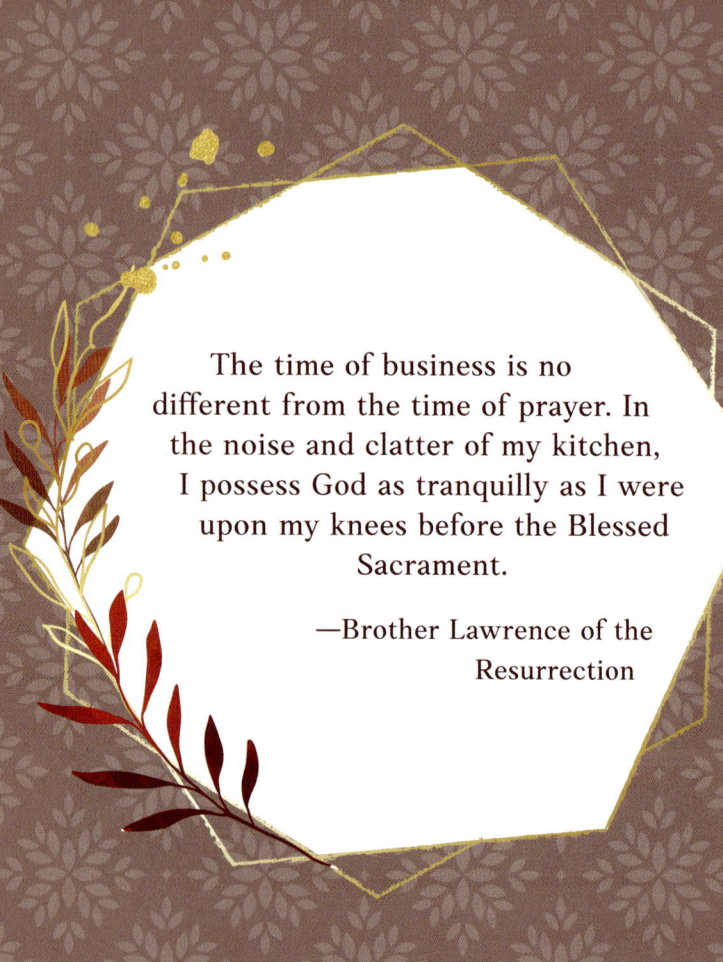

The time of business is no different from the time of prayer. In the noise and clatter of my kitchen, I possess God as tranquilly as I were upon my knees before the Blessed Sacrament.

—Brother Lawrence of the Resurrection

So will I sing praise unto thy name for ever, that I may daily perform my vows.

—Psalm 61:8

Please help me to draw closer to you, Lord, each and every day. Instill in me the desire to pray each day, to praise your name even on those gray and dreary days when I don't want to make an effort.

All night, all day

Angels watching over me, my Lord.

All night, all day

Angels watching over me.

—Traditional spiritual

Blessed be the Lord, who daily loadeth us with benefits, even the God of our salvation.

—Psalm 68:19

You grant your blessings, Lord, every day. The blessings of food, family, and faith. The blessings of natural beauty and human ingenuity. The blessing of life itself. Let me remember to thank you, every day.

Night and day may we give you praise and thanks, because you have shown us that all things belong to you, and all blessings are gifts from you.

—Clement of Alexandria

Give perfection to beginners, O Father; give intelligence to the little ones; give aid to those who are running their course. Give sorrow to the negligent; give fervor of spirit to the lukewarm. Give to the perfect a good consummation; for the sake of Christ Jesus our Lord.

—Early Christian prayer

I will both lay me down in peace,
and sleep: for thou, Lord, only
makest me dwell in safety.

—Psalm 4:8

My mind won't shut down, God. I lie in bed awake, fretting over the things that didn't go quite right today, and my worries about tomorrow. I ask you to be with me in this moment, to help me let go of the past and my fears about the future. I'm safe in your hands.

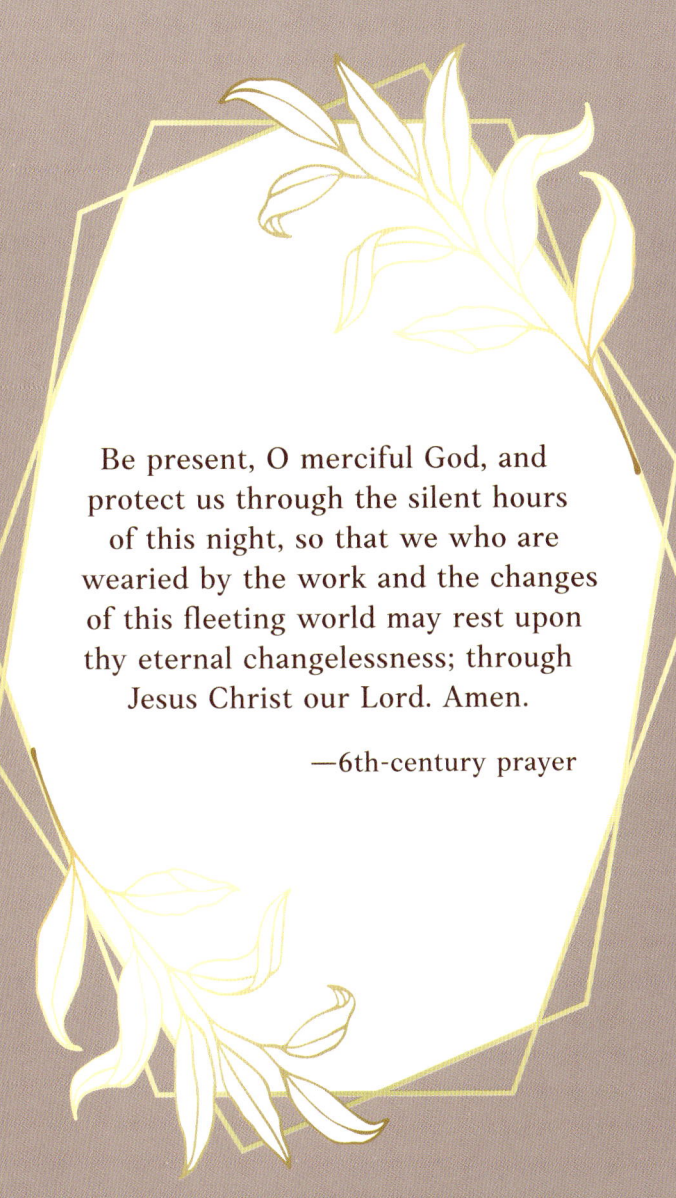

Be present, O merciful God, and protect us through the silent hours of this night, so that we who are wearied by the work and the changes of this fleeting world may rest upon thy eternal changelessness; through Jesus Christ our Lord. Amen.

—6th-century prayer

> Yet the Lord will command his loving kindness in the day time, and in the night his song shall be with me, and my prayer unto the God of my life.
>
> —Psalm 42:8

I don't have a trained voice, Lord, but you who created the sound of it are surely pleased when I raise it in song to you during my evening prayer. Let me take joy in song and prayer, delighting in your presence as you delight in mine.

Into thy
hands, O Father
and Lord, we commend
this night, ourselves, our families and friends, all those we love
and those who love us, all folk rightly
believing, and all who need thy pity
and protection: light us with thy holy
grace, and suffer us never to be separated from thee, O Lord in Trinity,
God everlasting.

—St. Edmund Rich

> Behold, he that keepeth Israel shall neither slumber nor sleep.
>
> —Psalm 121:4

As children, we used to sing, "He's got the whole world in his hands." Tonight as I go to sleep, let me rest peacefully in that assurance. I place my life in your hands, Father God, trusting in you to do what's best for me, for my family, for my friends, for the country, for the world.

Now the light has gone away;
Savior, listen while I pray.
Asking thee to watch and keep
And to send me quiet sleep.

Jesus, Savior, wash away
All that has been wrong today.
Help me every day to be
Good and gentle, more like thee.

Let my near and dear ones be
Always near and dear to thee.
O bring me and all I love
To thy happy home above. Amen.

—Traditional evening prayer

Let my prayer be set forth before thee as incense; and the lifting up of my hands as the evening sacrifice.

—Psalm 141:2

I lift up my hands to you, Lord, offering a sacrifice of praise. You've been with me every step of the way today, and I give you thanks for it.

God that
madest earth
and heaven,

darkness and light

Who the day for toil has given

For rest the night

Guard us waking, guard us sleeping

and when we die

May we in thy mighty keeping

All peaceful lie.

—Reginald
Heber

> Not my will, but thine, be done.
>
> —Luke 22:42

Father, I'm not facing what Jesus faced. But let his obedience be an example to me as I face smaller challenge. Let this be my prayer, every day of my life: not my will, but thine, be done.

May he support us all
the day long, till the shades
lengthen, and the evening comes,
and the busy world is hushed, and
the fever of life is over, and our work
is done! Then in his mercy may he give
us a safe lodging, and a holy rest, and
peace at the last.

—John Henry Newman

FORGIVENESS AND MERCY

God be merciful to me a sinner.

—Luke 18:13

Have mercy upon me, O God, according to thy lovingkindness: according unto the multitude of thy tender mercies blot out my transgressions.

Wash me throughly from mine iniquity, and cleanse me from my sin. For I acknowledge my transgressions: and my sin is ever before me.

Against thee, thee only, have I sinned, and done this evil in thy sight: that thou mightest be justified when thou speakest, and be clear when thou judgest.

Behold, I was shapen in iniquity; and in sin did my mother conceive me. Behold, thou desirest truth in the inward parts: and in the hidden part thou shalt make me to know wisdom.

Purge me with hyssop, and I shall be clean: wash me, and I shall be whiter than snow. Make me to hear joy and gladness; that the bones which thou hast broken may rejoice. Hide thy face from my sins, and blot out all mine iniquities.

Create in me a clean heart, O God; and renew a right spirit within me. Cast me not away from thy presence; and take not thy holy spirit from me. Restore unto me the joy of thy salvation; and uphold me with thy free spirit. Then will I teach transgressors thy ways; and sinners shall be converted unto thee.

Deliver me from bloodguiltiness, O God, thou God of my salvation: and my tongue shall sing aloud of thy righteousness. O Lord, open thou my lips; and my mouth shall shew forth thy praise. For thou desirest not sacrifice; else would I give it: thou delightest not in burnt offering. The sacrifices of God are a broken spirit: a broken and a contrite heart, O God, thou wilt not despise.

Do good in thy good pleasure unto Zion: build thou the walls of Jerusalem. Then shalt thou be pleased with the sacrifices of righteousness, with burnt offering and whole burnt offering: then shall they offer bullocks upon thine altar.

—Psalm 51

Forgive, O Lord, for thy dear Son

The ill that I this day have done.

That with the world, myself, and thee

I, ere I sleep, at peace may be.
Amen.

—Traditional prayer

> Truly God is good to Israel, even to such as are of a clean heart. But as for me, my feet were almost gone; my steps had well nigh slipped. For I was envious at the foolish, when I saw the prosperity of the wicked.
>
> —Psalm 73:1–3

Lord, when I see other people do wrong things and face no consequences, I get tempted myself. Why bother playing by the ethical rules at my job, when other people get ahead by cutting corners? Why bother being rigidly honest on my taxes? Why not be a little dishonest in my personal relationships, if it will make things easier? Further down in Psalm 73, the psalmist says, "Behold, these are the ungodly, who prosper in the world; they increase in riches. Verily I have cleansed my heart in vain" (12–13). Centuries later, I recognize that feeling! The psalmist goes to the sanctuary of God to restore his faith. Let me do the same, remembering to keep my heart clean for you.

How long wilt thou forget me, O Lord? for ever? how long wilt thou hide thy face from me? How long shall I take counsel in my soul, having sorrow in my heart daily? how long shall mine enemy be exalted over me?

—Psalm 13:1–2

Lord, you know that I'm going through a hard time, and it's hard to keep the faith. It's hard to keep on praying when I feel distant from you, like you've forgotten me. Please help me remember your goodness, your mercy, and your salvation.

> Thou hast set our iniquities before thee, our secret sins in the light of thy countenance.
>
> —Psalm 90:8

A friend from church told me recently that she saw me as an example. It humbled me, because I know how far that is from the truth. I put on a good face in public, but inside, I grumble. I hold onto grudges and resentments. I judge people harshly—especially when I'm jealous of them. I may seem holy on the outside, but you see the inside, Father, even when I don't want you to. Please forgive those iniquities and give me a clean heart and the strength to do better.

Then said Jesus, Father, forgive them; for they know not what they do.

—Luke 23:34

Lord, let me forgive as you forgave: generously, freely, and totally.

Out of the depths have I cried unto thee, O Lord. Lord, hear my voice: let thine ears be attentive to the voice of my supplications. If thou, Lord, shouldest mark iniquities, O Lord, who shall stand? But there is forgiveness with thee, that thou mayest be feared.

—Psalm 130:1–4

Jesus told a judgmental crowd that the person without sin should cast the first stone. We're all sinners when seen by God—but God loves us and chooses to forgive and extend mercy. What a great gift!

Lord, who shall abide in thy tabernacle? who shall dwell in thy holy hill? He that walketh uprightly, and worketh righteousness, and speaketh the truth in his heart. He that backbiteth not with his tongue, nor doeth evil to his neighbour, nor taketh up a reproach against his neighbour.

—Psalm 15:1–3

Oh, Lord, please help me to control my tongue. It can be tempting to pass along gossip, sometimes even under the guise of concern. Let me avoid doing wrong with my words by passing along rumors or harmful truths.

> Search me, O God, and know my heart: try me, and know my thoughts: And see if there be any wicked way in me, and lead me in the way everlasting.
>
> —Psalm 139:23–24

Sometimes we want to hide from our sins, and hide our sins from God. But there is freedom in acknowledging our sins, for then God can teach us, forgive us, and help us choose his ways.

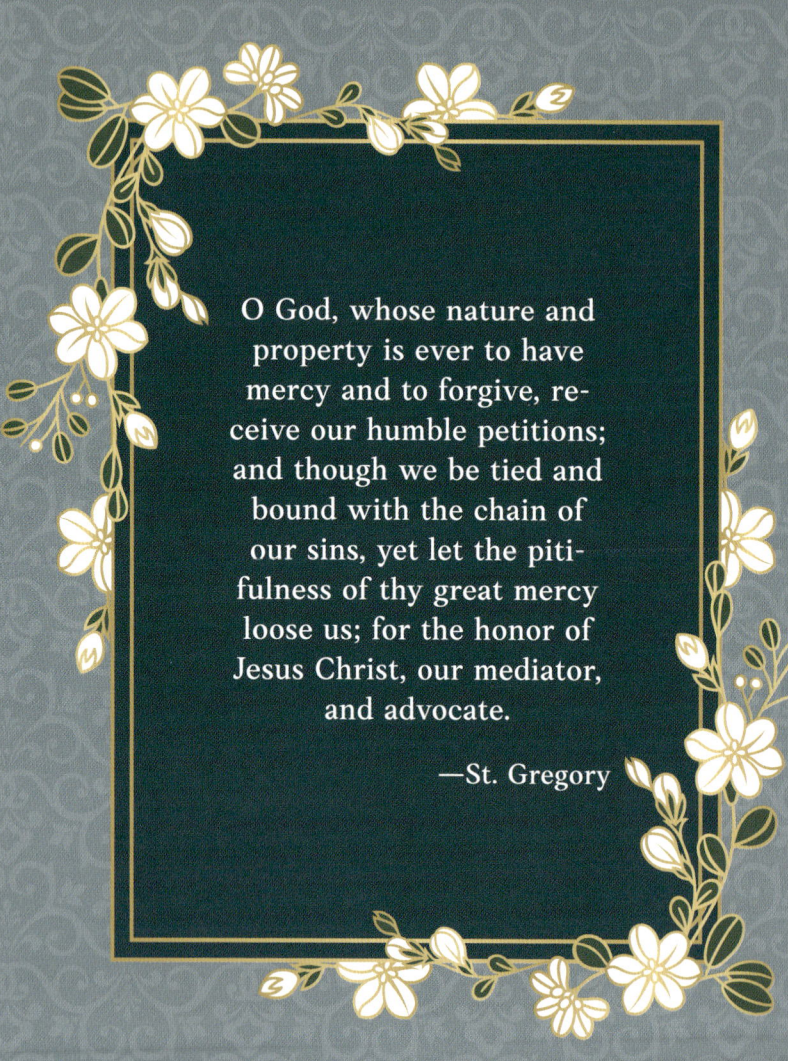

O God, whose nature and property is ever to have mercy and to forgive, receive our humble petitions; and though we be tied and bound with the chain of our sins, yet let the pitifulness of thy great mercy loose us; for the honor of Jesus Christ, our mediator, and advocate.

—St. Gregory

Cleanse thou me from secret faults. Keep back thy servant also from presumptuous sins; let them not have dominion over me: then shall I be upright, and I shall be innocent from the great transgression. Let the words of my mouth, and the meditation of my heart, be acceptable in thy sight, O Lord, my strength, and my redeemer.

—Psalm 19:12–14

Dear Lord and Father of humankind,

Forgive our foolish ways;

Reclothe us in our rightful mind,

In purer lives thy service find,

In deeper reverence, praise.

—John Greenleaf Whittier

> Who shall ascend into the hill of the Lord? or who shall stand in his holy place? He that hath clean hands, and a pure heart; who hath not lifted up his soul unto vanity, nor sworn deceitfully.
>
> —Psalm 24:3–4

Lord, thank you for your Word, which is clear about the behavior that pleases you. When I falter and fail, as you know I do, I can always return to your Word for reminders, guidelines, and fortification.

O lord, thou hast searched me, and known me. Thou knowest my downsitting and mine uprising, thou understandest my thought afar off. Thou compassest my path and my lying down, and art acquainted with all my ways.

—Psalm 139:1–3

You know my ways, and that includes my flaws. You know my darkest tendencies and sins—and you love me anyway! Lord, thank you for your everlasting love and forgiveness.

I will sing of the mercies of the
Lord forever,

I will sing, I will sing,

I will sing of the mercies of the
Lord forever,

I will sing of the mercies of the Lord.

With my mouth will I make known
thy faithfulness, thy faithfulness,

With my mouth will I make known
thy faithfulness to all generations,

I will sing of the mercies of the
Lord forever,

I will sing of the mercies of the Lord.

—James H. Fillmore

> The Lord is merciful and gracious, slow to anger, and plenteous in mercy.
>
> —Psalm 103:8

We cannot match God's mercy, but we can use it as our model. We can choose to let go of our anger when it rises up quickly. We can choose to look kindly at others. We can choose to extend mercy to others, as it has been extended to us.

> Remember, O Lord, thy tender mercies and thy lovingkindnesses; for they have been ever of old. Remember not the sins of my youth, nor my transgressions: according to thy mercy remember thou me for thy goodness' sake, O Lord. Good and upright is the Lord: therefore will he teach sinners in the way.
>
> —Psalm 25:6–8

I'm still learning, Lord, after all these years. I hope that I'm not as prideful or impatient as when I was young, but I know I still need to guard against those tendencies. Thank you, Lord, for teaching me your ways, over and over again, throughout my life.

Such as sit in darkness and in the shadow of death, being bound in affliction and iron; Because they rebelled against the words of God, and contemned the counsel of the most High: Therefore he brought down their heart with labour; they fell down, and there was none to help. Then they cried unto the Lord in their trouble, and he saved them out of their distresses.

—Psalm 107:10–13

Short-term, turning away from God seems to bring happiness. Long-term, it does not. Thank you, Father, for saving me from distress—even the distress I bring upon myself.

Jesus, Lord, remember me when thou comest into thy kingdom.

—Luke 23:42

It's never too late to turn to God. The Bible tells the stories of the two men crucified on either side of Jesus, and how one of them turned to him and defended him against the accusations of the other. Today, the words of that repentant sinner are the words of my own prayer.

Set a watch, O Lord, before my mouth; keep the door of my lips. Incline not my heart to any evil thing, to practise wicked works with men that work iniquity: and let me not eat of their dainties.

—Psalm 141:3–4

Lord, I ask you to surround me with people who do good works and speak kind and truthful words. My choice of friends and associates can affect my own behavior, and it's easier to resist temptation and sin when I am not exposed to it.

> For thy name's sake, O Lord, pardon mine iniquity; for it is great.
>
> —Psalm 25:11

Father, you know my shame and misery. You know how I stumbled and fell. You know my reasons and justifications, my regrets and my sorrows. You know my sincere repentence. I ask you to forgive me now.

There's a wideness in God's mercy,

Like the wideness of the sea.

There's a kindness in God's justice,

Which is more than liberty.

There is welcome for the sinner,

And more graces for the good.

There is mercy with the Savior,

There is healing in his blood.

—Frederick William Faber

> Sing unto the Lord, O ye saints of his, and give thanks at the remembrance of his holiness. For his anger endureth but a moment; in his favour is life: weeping may endure for a night, but joy cometh in the morning.
>
> —Psalm 30:4–5

You have forgiven me! I prayed yesterday for forgiveness, and today I feel fresh and new. Your mercy is indeed great, Lord, and I feel the joy of a fresh start this morning.

I cried by reason of mine affliction unto the Lord, and he heard me; out of the belly of hell cried I, and thou heardest my voice.

For thou hadst cast me into the deep, in the midst of the seas; and the floods compassed me about: all thy billows and thy waves passed over me.

Then I said, I am cast out of thy sight; yet I will look again toward thy holy temple.

The waters compassed me about, even to the soul: the depth closed me round about, the weeds were wrapped about my head.

I went down to the bottoms of the mountains; the earth with her bars was about me for ever: yet hast thou brought up my life from corruption, O Lord my God.

When my soul fainted within me I remembered the Lord: and my prayer came in unto thee, into thine holy temple.

They that observe lying vanities forsake their own mercy.

But I will sacrifice unto thee with the voice of thanksgiving; I will pay that that I have vowed. Salvation is of the Lord.

—Jonah 2:2-9

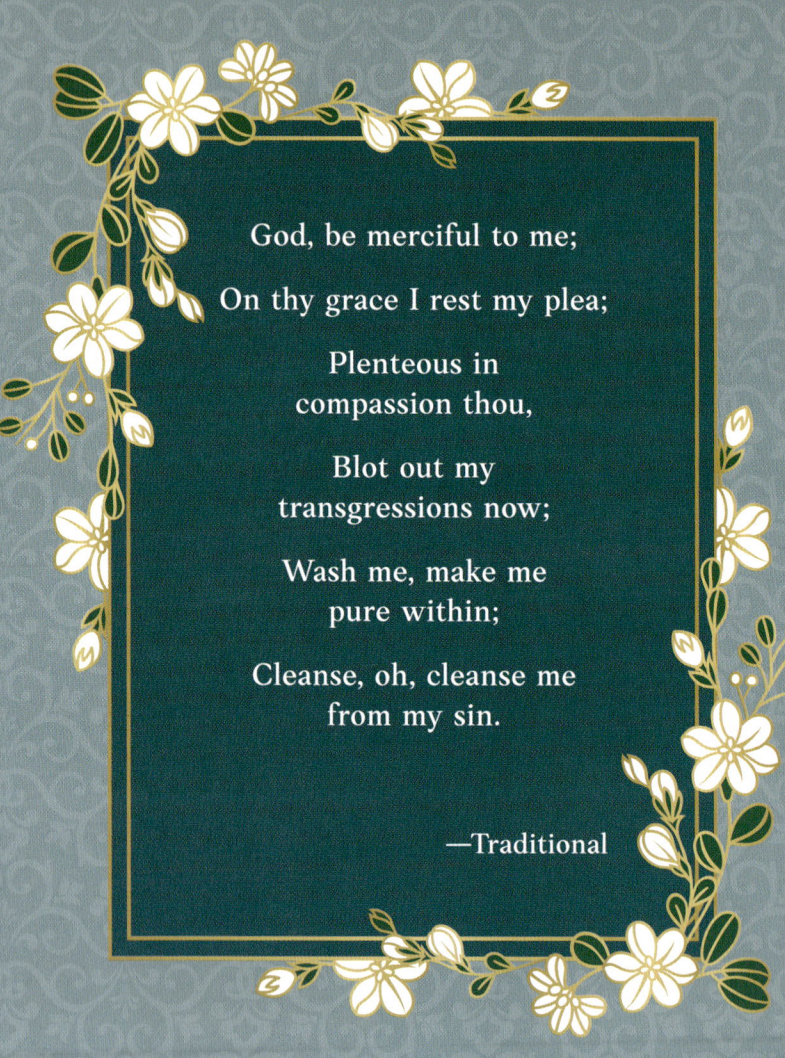

God, be merciful to me;

On thy grace I rest my plea;

Plenteous in compassion thou,

Blot out my transgressions now;

Wash me, make me pure within;

Cleanse, oh, cleanse me from my sin.

—Traditional

> Thou hast forgiven the iniquity of thy people, thou hast covered all their sin.
>
> —Psalm 85:2

Today I pray not only for myself, but for those I love. Please help my friends and family members to draw close to you. Please guide my children on the right paths. Please help our political and moral leaders choose rightly when faced with difficult decisions. We all need your mercy, Lord, and your forgiveness.

Blessed is he whose transgression is forgiven, whose sin is covered. Blessed is the man unto whom the Lord imputeth not iniquity, and in whose spirit there is no guile. When I kept silence, my bones waxed old through my roaring all the day long. For day and night thy hand was heavy upon me: my moisture is turned into the drought of summer. Selah.

I acknowledge my sin unto thee, and mine iniquity have I not hid. I said, I will confess my transgressions unto the Lord; and thou forgavest the iniquity of my sin. Selah.

For this shall every one that is godly pray unto thee in a time when thou mayest be found: surely in the floods of great waters they shall not come nigh unto him. Thou art my hiding place; thou shalt preserve me from trouble; thou shalt compass me about with songs of deliverance. Selah.

I will instruct thee and teach thee in the way which thou shalt go: I will guide thee with mine eye. Be ye not as the horse, or as the mule, which have no understanding: whose mouth must be held in with bit and bridle, lest they come near unto thee. Many sorrows shall be to the wicked: but he that trusteth in the Lord, mercy shall compass him about. Be glad in the Lord, and rejoice, ye righteous: and shout for joy, all ye that are upright in heart.

—Psalm 32

What can wash away my sin?

Nothing but the blood of Jesus.

What can make me whole again?

Nothing but the blood of Jesus.

O precious is the flow

That makes me white as snow;

No other fount I know;

Nothing but the blood of Jesus.

—Robert Lowry

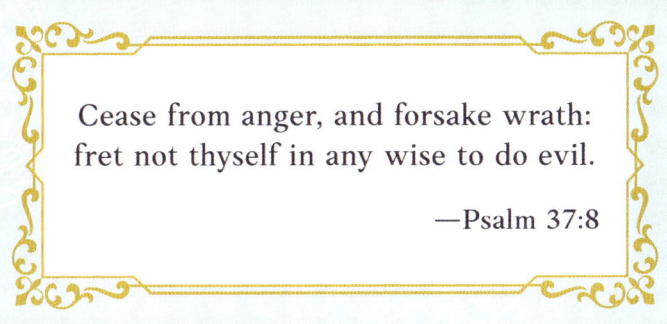

> Cease from anger, and forsake wrath: fret not thyself in any wise to do evil.
>
> —Psalm 37:8

Deliver me from anger, Lord. Deliver me from the urge to spit cruel words and score points, to win my way at the expense of treating others with respect and kindness. Curb my tongue. Help me let go of this anger and choose peace and mercy instead.

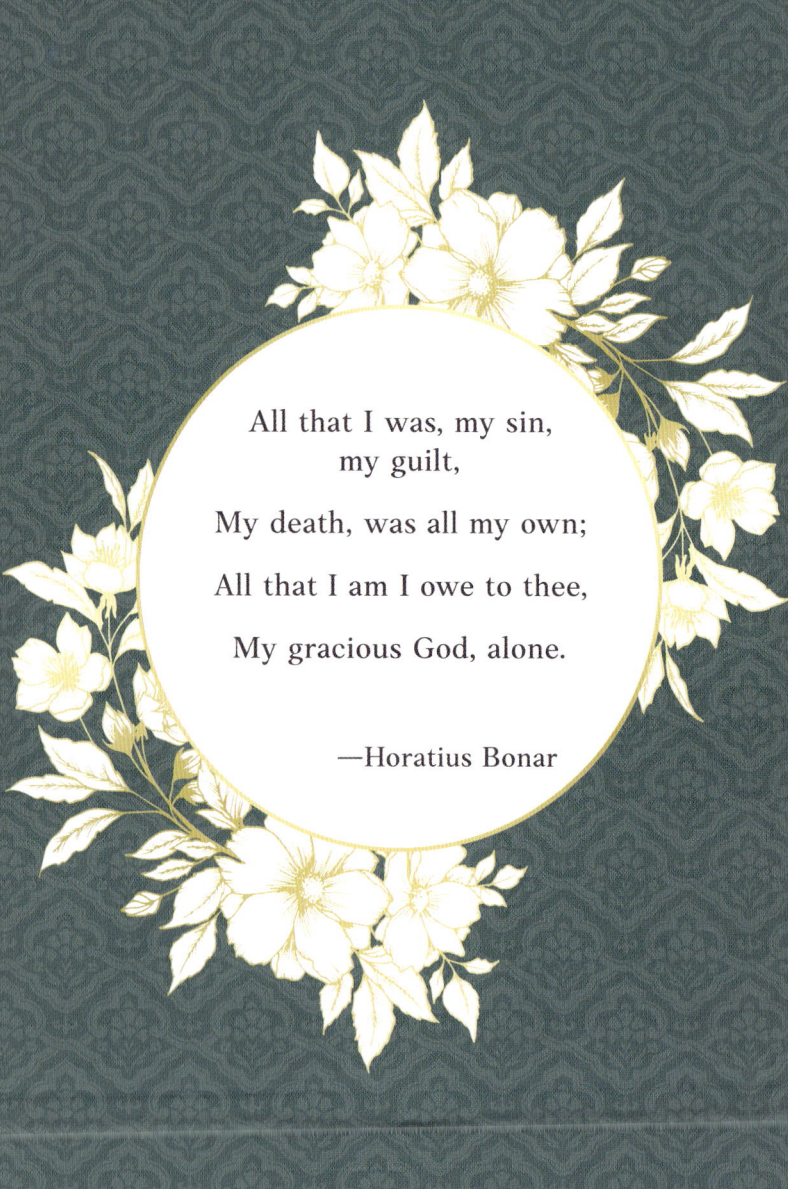

All that I was, my sin, my guilt,

My death, was all my own;

All that I am I owe to thee,

My gracious God, alone.

—Horatius Bonar

> For I will declare mine iniquity; I will be sorry for my sin.
>
> —Psalm 38:18

Lord, I need to ask a friend for forgiveness. I'm nervous about it. Please help me acknowledge my wrongs without giving excuses, and please help me to make things right. Please smooth the pathway between us, so we can restore our relationship.

Take ev'ry sin to Jesus,
Who died on Calv'ry's tree,
For he will freely pardon,
And give you liberty.
Take ev'ry sin to Jesus,
Before his altar bow;
Take ev'ry sin to Jesus,
And he will save you now.

—Oswald J. Smith

Withhold not thou thy tender mercies from me, O Lord: let thy lovingkindness and thy truth continually preserve me. For innumerable evils have compassed me about: mine iniquities have taken hold upon me, so that I am not able to look up; they are more than the hairs of mine head: therefore my heart faileth me.

—Psalm 40:11–12

Please restore my heart, Lord. Heal me in body, mind, soul, heart, and spirit. Thank you.

FAITH

And the apostles said unto the Lord, Increase our faith. And the Lord said, If ye had faith as a grain of mustard seed, ye might say unto this sycamine tree, Be thou plucked up by the root, and be thou planted in the sea; and it should obey you.

—Luke 17:5–6

We walk by faith, and not by sight;
No gracious words we hear
From him who spoke as none ne'er spoke,
But we believe him near.

We may not touch his hands and side,
Nor follow where he trod;
But in his promise we rejoice,
And cry, "My Lord and God!"

Help then, O Lord, our unbelief;
And may our faith abound,
To call on you when you are near,
And seek where you are found.

That when our lives of faith
are done,
In realms of clearer light,
We may behold you as you are,
With full and endless sight.

—Henry Alford

> Thy mercy, O Lord, is in the heavens; and thy faithfulness reacheth unto the clouds.
>
> —Psalm 36:5

Father God, you are continually faithful to me. I can't fathom the immensity of your faithfulness and love. Please help me grow in my faithfulness to you.

Teach us, good Lord, to serve thee as thou deservest.
To give and not to count the cost: To fight and not to heed the wounds: To toil and not to seek for rest: To labour and not to ask for any reward save that of knowing that we do thy will.

—St. Ignatius of Loyola

> And straightway the father of the child cried out, and said with tears, Lord, I believe; help thou mine unbelief.
>
> —Mark 9:24

My faith is not always as steady and unwavering as I would like. You know that, Lord. Yet I can say with this man from the Bible: I do believe. But where I fall short, where I falter, help my unbelief.

> I have not hid thy righteousness within my heart; I have declared thy faithfulness and thy salvation: I have not concealed thy lovingkindness and thy truth from the great congregation.
>
> —Psalm 40:10

I've learned that being part of a community of faith helps my faith grow. While I need private, one-on-one time with God, my faith increases when I hear friends telling stories of how God works in their lives. Talking about God helps me truly appreciate his work in my life as well. Lord, please help me always proclaim your love and witness to your works in a way that helps increase the faith of others!

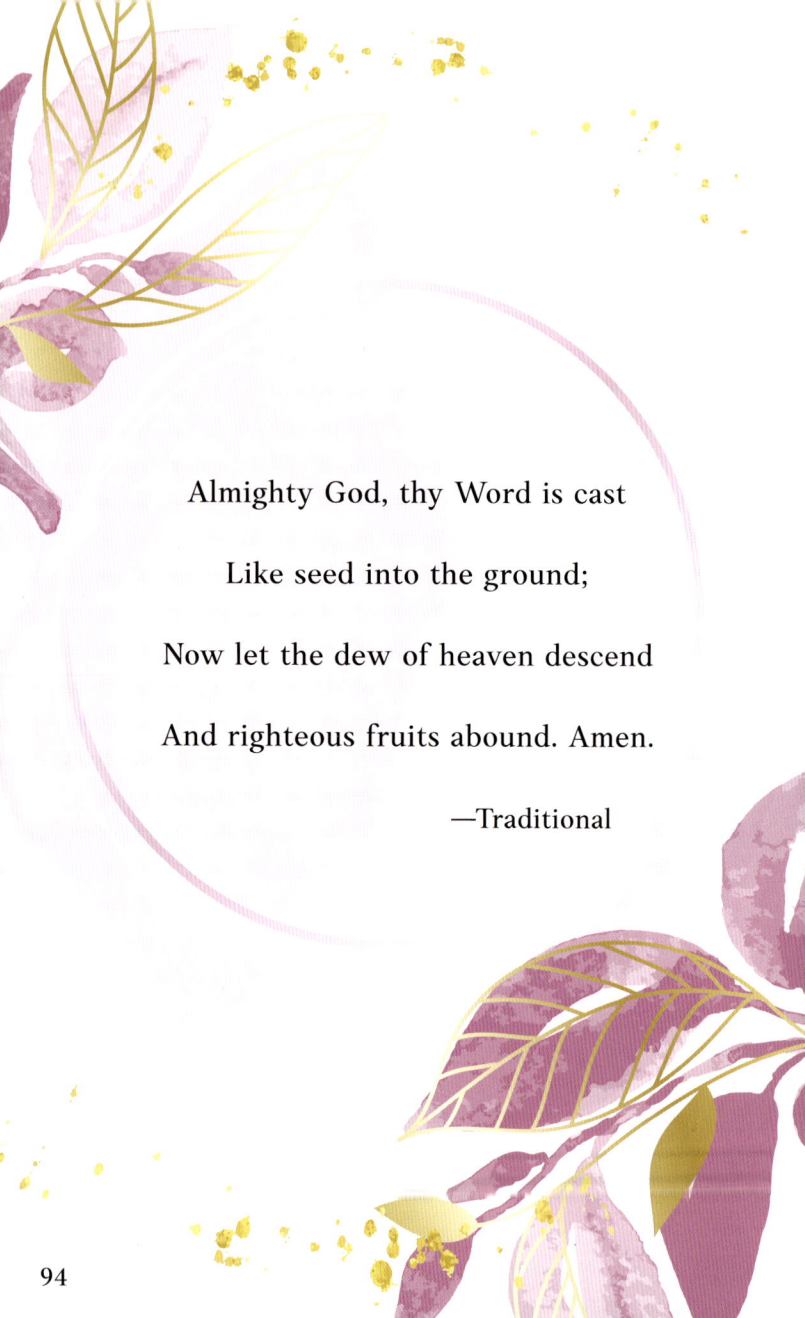

Almighty God, thy Word is cast

Like seed into the ground;

Now let the dew of heaven descend

And righteous fruits abound. Amen.

—Traditional

He hath remembered his covenant for ever, the word which he commanded to a thousand generations. Which covenant he made with Abraham, and his oath unto Isaac.

—Psalm 105:8–9

Faith sometimes means giving back to God the things and people we cherish most. Abraham's faith was tested, and his response has become a model of faith for all believers.

> I know, O Lord, that thy judgments are right, and that thou in faithfulness hast afflicted me.
>
> —Psalm 119:75

Lord, I don't always know why you let things happen. But I resolve to have faith in you, that you can draw good out of events that seem evil or senseless to me. I trust, too, that when I fail to do right and suffer the consequences, you want to help me back to the right pathway.

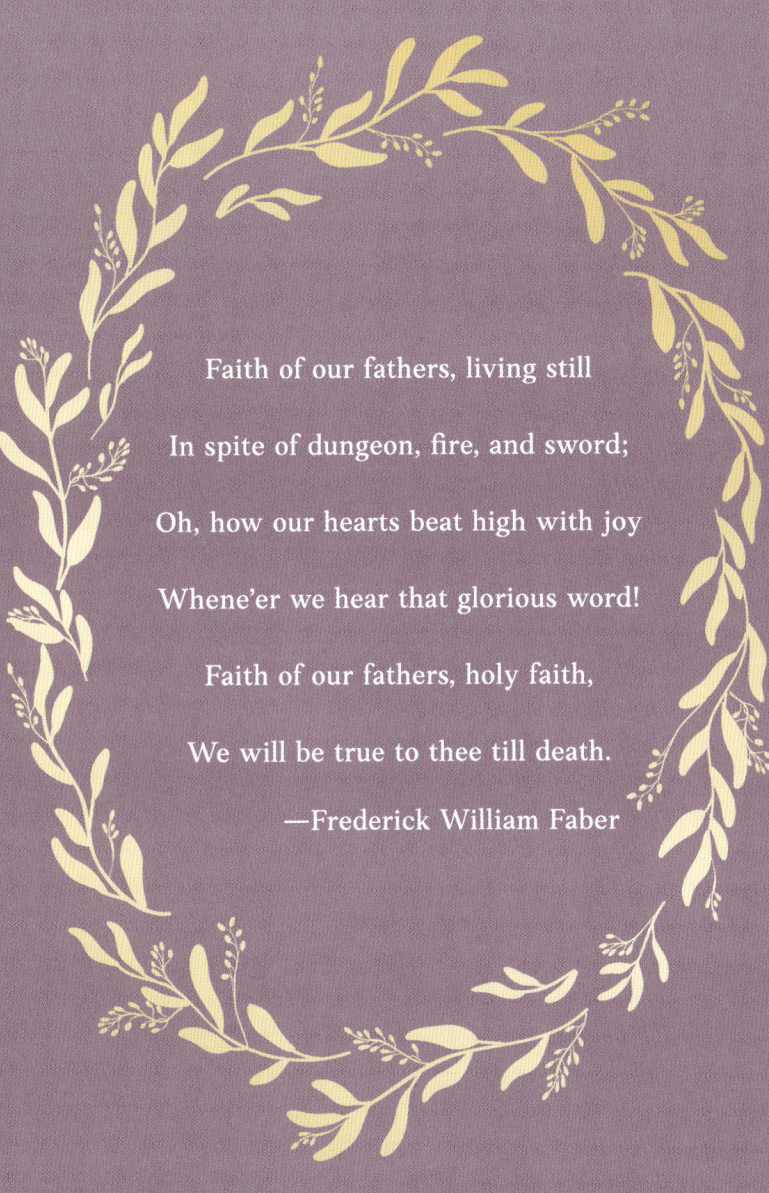

Faith of our fathers, living still

In spite of dungeon, fire, and sword;

Oh, how our hearts beat high with joy

Whene'er we hear that glorious word!

Faith of our fathers, holy faith,

We will be true to thee till death.

—Frederick William Faber

O love the Lord, all ye his saints: for the Lord preserveth the faithful, and plentifully rewardeth the proud doer.

—Psalm 31:23

I want to be faithful, Lord! I want to grow in faith and reap the spiritual rewards that come from that. I want the deep faith that my mother and grandmother had, which granted them resilience in facing life's problems. Thank you!

My faith has found a resting place,

Not in device nor creed.

I trust the ever-living One;

His wounds for me shall plead.

I need no other argument,

I need no other plea,

It is enough that Jesus died,

And that he died for me.

—E. E. Hewitt

My God, my God, why hast thou forsaken me? why art thou so far from helping me, and from the words of my roaring?

—Psalm 22:1

If our faith was never tested, how would we know we had any? When things go wrong and we can still say, "I believe in God no matter what happens," we show our faith to be real.

> For he hath not despised nor abhorred the affliction of the afflicted; neither hath he hid his face from him; but when he cried unto him, he heard.
>
> —Psalm 22:24

Psalm 22, which Jesus said while on the Cross, begins as a lament. It ends as a statement of faith. Sometimes I do not think you hear my cries, Lord. You seem to have abandoned me. Like the psalmist, I can acknowledge that feeling while still resolving to have faith.

> Mine eyes shall be upon the faithful of the land, that they may dwell with me: he that walketh in a perfect way, he shall serve me.
>
> —Psalm 101:6

Faith requires personal commitment, decision, and purpose. God sets the plan, but we must do the legwork.

Hear my prayer, O Lord, give ear to my supplications: in thy faithfulness answer me, and in thy righteousness.

—Psalm 143:1

Even in our toughest moments, Lord, we yearn to grow into fullest flower. Give us a faith as resilient and determined as dandelions pushing up through cracks in the pavement.

My faith looks up to thee,

Thou Lamb of Calvary,

Savior divine!

Now hear me while I pray,

Take all my guilt away;

O let me from this day

Be wholly thine.

—Ray Palmer

> If ye have faith as a grain of mustard seed, ye shall say unto this mountain, Remove hence to yonder place; and it shall remove; and nothing shall be impossible unto you.
>
> —Matthew 17:20

Faith has moved mountains, healed hearts, and saved men from the sword. With this power we need not search for answers outside of the Lord.

I will sing of the mercies of the Lord for ever: with my mouth will I make known thy faithfulness to all generations.

For I have said, Mercy shall be built up for ever: thy faithfulness shalt thou establish in the very heavens.

I have made a covenant with my chosen, I have sworn unto David my servant,

Thy seed will I establish for ever, and build up thy throne to all generations. Selah.

And the heavens shall praise thy wonders, O Lord: thy faithfulness also in the congregation of the saints.

For who in the heaven can be compared unto the Lord? who among the sons of the mighty can be likened unto the Lord?

God is greatly to be feared in the assembly of the saints, and to be had in reverence of all them that are about him.

O Lord God of hosts, who is a strong Lord like unto thee? or to thy faithfulness round about thee?

—Psalm 89:1–8

For
thou art great,
and doest wondrous
things: thou art God alone.

—Psalm 86:10

Faith thrives when we stay focused on God rather than on ourselves.

> For thou hast girded me
> with strength unto the battle: thou hast
> subdued under me those that rose up
> against me.
>
> —Psalm 18:39

When a task requiring faith confronts us, voices around us may say, "It can't be done." The voice may even come from within us, and we may want to quit before we start. But if we hold on to faith, we can succeed, no matter what the critics say.

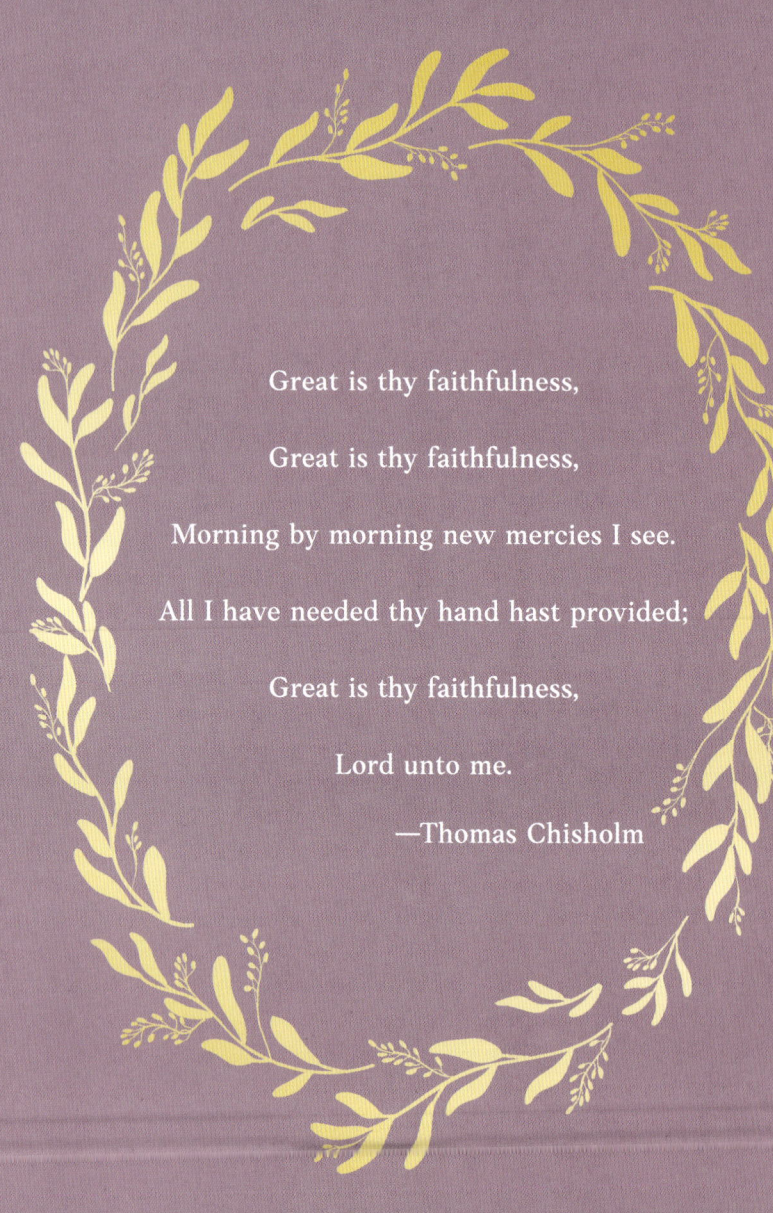

Great is thy faithfulness,

Great is thy faithfulness,

Morning by morning new mercies I see.

All I have needed thy hand hast provided;

Great is thy faithfulness,

Lord unto me.

—Thomas Chisholm

> Cast me not off in the time of old age;
> forsake me not when my strength faileth.
>
> —Psalm 71:9

Aging doesn't necessitate letting go of faith. Even though our bodies are getting older and our thinking may not be as sharp as it once was, God is still the same. We can always depend on him.

The steps of a good man are ordered by the Lord: and he delighteth in his way.

—Psalm 37:23

When we step out and do the thing we believe God wants us to do, even if it doesn't make sense, that's faith. Our greatest rewards can come from those acts.

Living by faith in Jesus above,

Trusting, confiding in his great love;

From all harm safe in his sheltering arm,

I'm living by faith and feel no alarm.

—James Wells

But let all those that put their trust in thee rejoice: let them ever shout for joy, because thou defendest them: let them also that love thy name be joyful in thee.

—Psalm 5:11

We can maintain our joy when we remember how faithful and unchanging God is. Focusing on him brings renewed joy.

Oh, for a faith that will not shrink
Though pressed by many a foe,
That will not tremble on the brink
Of poverty or woe:

It will not murmur nor complain
Beneath the chast'ning rod,
But in the hour of grief or pain
Can lean upon its God:

A faith that shines more bright and clear
When tempests rage without,
That, when in danger, knows no fear;
In darkness feels no doubt.

—Henry Alford

LOVE

Jesus, friend of the poor,

Feeder of the hungry,

Healer of the sick,

I adore thee.

—*A Book of Prayers for Students*

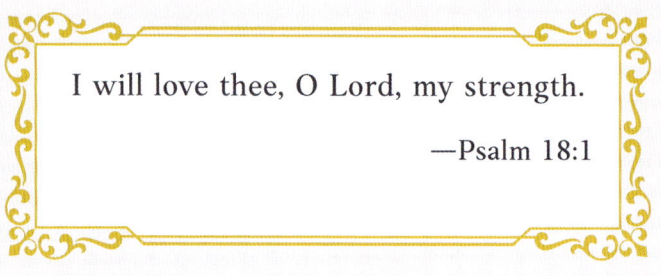

> I will love thee, O Lord, my strength.
>
> —Psalm 18:1

God, when I feel weak, I turn to you. When I feel scared, I turn to you. When I feel hopeless, I turn to you. You are my strength, my consolation, and my hope.

O love of God, how rich and pure!

How measureless and strong!

It shall forevermore endure—

The saints' and angels' song.

—Frederick Lehman

> The Lord openeth the eyes of the blind: the Lord raiseth them that are bowed down: the Lord loveth the righteous: The Lord preserveth the strangers; he relieveth the fatherless and widow: but the way of the wicked he turneth upside down.
>
> —Psalm 146:8–9

Lord, thank you for the good gifts you have given me! Thank you for your love, which has healed my soul of emotional wounds, bolstered me during difficult times, and guided me as I've made decisions. You are truly generous.

Then Jesus beholding him loved him, and said unto him, One thing thou lackest: go thy way, sell whatsoever thou hast, and give to the poor, and thou shalt have treasure in heaven: and come, take up the cross, and follow me.

—Mark 10:21

Lord, you love us, and because of that love, you want us to be righteous. You want to share eternal life with us, and so you tell us to take up our cross and follow you.

> For thy lovingkindness is before mine eyes: and I have walked in thy truth.
>
> —Psalm 26:3

We love because you love us, God. We try to follow your example of enduring, faithful, abiding love. The more we love others, the kinder we are to each other, the more we are like you.

Love divine, all loves excelling,

Joy of Heav'n to Earth come down,

Fix in us thy humble dwelling,

All thy faithful mercies crown;

Jesus, thou art all compassion,

Pure, unbounded love thou art;

Visit us with thy salvation,

Enter ev'ry trembling heart.

—Charles Wesley

> I love the Lord, because he hath heard my voice and my supplications.
>
> —Psalm 116:1

God is the great listener. Even the best-intentioned people sometimes misunderstand others, or don't want to hear about their problems and struggles because it will bring them down. God is always there, however, listening and loving.

> Beloved, let us love one another: for love is of God; and every one that loveth is born of God, and knoweth God.
>
> —1 John 4:7

Lord, please hear my prayer today: I want to be more loving. I want to see others as you do, and love them as you do.

> Lord, I have loved the habitation of thy house, and the place where thine honour dwelleth.
>
> —Psalm 26:8

Lord, thank you for bringing me to my current church home. When I moved here, I visited several places before finding a community of believers where I felt I fit in. With this group of people, I feel like we're on a journey together, to seek you and grow in faith and love.

Jesus loves me so,

Jesus loves me so,

I will love him more and more,

For Jesus loves me so.

—William H. Flaville

Ye that love the Lord, hate evil: he preserveth the souls of his saints; he delivereth them out of the hand of the wicked. Light is sown for the righteous, and gladness for the upright in heart.

—Psalm 97:10–11

Lord, I want to be righteous. I want to make good choices and turn away from evil. You know that I fail sometimes: I convince myself that a sin is not a big deal, and fall into laxness. Please restore my fervor to follow you, seeking always this promise of the light and gladness that only come from following you.

And Mary said, My soul doth magnify the Lord, And my spirit hath rejoiced in God my Saviour For he hath regarded the low estate of his handmaiden: for, behold, from henceforth all generations shall call me blessed. For he that is mighty hath done to me great things; and holy is his name.

—Luke 1:46–49

Lord, let me do your will like Mary did. Let me see your work in my life and praise and thank you for it. I don't always recognize it, but when I do pay attention, I see how you love me and shower blessings on me. Let me rejoice in you in turn.

> And I will delight myself in thy commandments, which I have loved.
>
> —Psalm 119:47

The deeper the relationship I have with God, the more I appreciate his Word. Scripture comes alive, with verses that I've heard a hundred times suddenly kindling and catching fire in my heart. Please continue to give me a better understanding of the Bible, and a bigger love.

My Jesus, I love thee, I know thou art mine;

For thee all the follies of sin I resign;

My gracious Redeemer, my Savior art thou;

If ever I loved thee, my Jesus, 'tis now.

—James Duffell and William Featherston

> Because thy lovingkindness is better than life, my lips shall praise thee.
>
> —Psalm 63:3

You love me! What an amazing gift that is! How can I respond except with praise, thanksgiving, and awe?

> And now, Israel, what doth
> the Lord thy God require of thee,
> but to fear the Lord thy God, to
> walk in all his ways, and to love him,
> and to serve the Lord thy God with
> all thy heart and with all thy soul.
>
> —Deuteronomy 10:12

I don't always put you first, God, but I know that's the goal: to love you with an all-encompassing love that directs all my actions. Please help me let you into my heart fully and completely, withholding nothing.

Look thou upon me, and
be merciful unto me, as
thou usest to do unto those
that love thy name.

—Psalm 119:132

Oh God, I need your help now. I ask you to have mercy on me and heal me from all my hurts, physical and spiritual and emotional. I ask you to free me from the pain that is making your love seem distant and unreal. Above all, whatever the outcome of this prayer, let me please have faith in your love.

Oh, the deep, deep love of Jesus—

Vast, unmeasured, boundless, free—

Rolling as a mighty ocean

In its fullness over me!

Underneath me, all around me

Is the current of his love—

Leading onward, leading homeward

To his glorious rest above.

—S. Trevor Francis

Let all those that seek thee rejoice and be glad in thee: let such as love thy salvation say continually, The Lord be magnified.

—Psalm 40:16

We sang a hymn of praise in church today, Lord, and the choir raised the rafters! What a blessing, to be in company with fellow believers in a circle of love for you and each other.

And all the days of Enoch were three hundred sixty and five years: And Enoch walked with God: and he was not; for God took him.

—Genesis 5:23–24

May I please you, Lord, like Enoch did, walking in your ways, seeking to be close to you.

> Because he hath set his love upon me, therefore will I deliver him: I will set him on high, because he hath known my name.
>
> —Psalm 91:14

This psalm contains a series of beautiful promises: that no evil will befall believers, that angels have charge of us, that we shall be in danger from lions and snakes but shall not be harmed. You promise to reward those who love you, God. Let me love you not only because of the promise of reward, though, but out of gratitude for the love you have given me.

What wondrous love is this,
O my soul, O my soul!

What wondrous love is this,
O my soul!

What wondrous love is this,
that caused the Lord of bliss

To bear the dreadful curse for
my soul, for my soul,

To bear the dreadful curse for
my soul.

—Traditional

> Therefore I love thy commandments above gold; yea, above fine gold.
>
> —Psalm 119:127

On a metaphorical level, we're asked to prize God's Word over treasure, to treat it as a precious. On a literal level, following God's commandments doesn't necessarily result in wealth. In fact, the Bible warns in several places against putting the quest for money over the desire to do God's will. Let me love you and follow you, God, regardless of my financial circumstances, seeking out your Word over fame or power.

Be perfect, be of good comfort, be of one mind, live in peace; and the God of love and peace shall be with you.

—2 Corinthians 13:11

We're asked to love God and love others. When we love God, love of others naturally flows from that, smoothing over arguments and disagreements. We may not always think exactly the same way, but we can still live in peace and harmony.

Shew thy marvellous lovingkindness,
O thou that savest by thy right hand
them which put their trust in thee
from those that rise up against them.

—Psalm 17:7

You want to help us, Lord. You want to save us. You want us to trust in you, so that you can do great things for us. You want to share your lovingkindness; we just need to let you

Lord, grant me a simple, kind, open, believing, loving and generous heart, worthy of being your dwelling place.

—John Sergieff

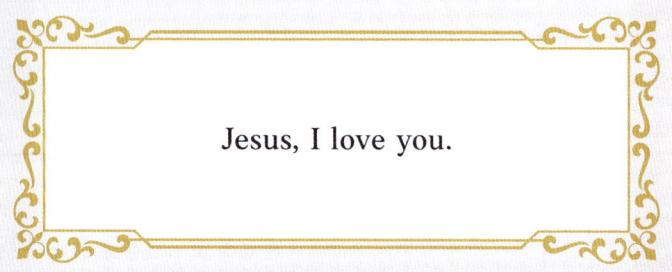

Jesus, I love you.

Take my life, and let it be

Consecrated, Lord, to thee;

Take my moments and my days;

Let them flow in ceaseless praise.

Take my hands, and let them move

At the impulse of thy love.

Take my feet, and let them be

Swift and beautiful for thee.

Take my love, my Lord, I pour

At thy feet its treasure store.

Take myself, and I will be

Ever, only, all for thee.

—Frances Ridley Havergal

Draw me completely into yourself,

So that I might completely melt in your love.

Lay upon me, stamp upon me,

So that my stubborn pride might be destroyed.

Embrace me, kiss me,

So that my spiritual ugliness may turn to beauty.

Lock me into your chamber,

So that I might never stray from your presence.

—Johann Freylinghausen

Hatred stirreth up strifes:
but love covereth all sins.

—Proverbs 10:12

Lord, I go through times when I get stressed out and everyone irritates me. My spouse's sense of humor gets on my nerves instead of amusing me; my colleagues don't do things according to my preferences; my friends send me texts that seem flippant and dismissive. When I'm in that kind of mood, please help me take a breath and let my irritations go, replacing them with love. Let me be charitable when I interpret the actions of others, hoping that they, and you, will extend that charity to me.

Open wide the window of
our spirits,

O Lord, and fill us full
of light;

Open wide the door of
our hearts,

That we may receive and
entertain thee

With all our powers of
adoration and love.

—Christina Rossetti

> The Lord hath appeared of old unto me, saying, Yea, I have loved thee with an everlasting love: therefore with lovingkindness have I drawn thee.
>
> —Jeremiah 31:3

God's love lasts. It doesn't ebb and flow, or diminish over time. Our love may waver, but God's steadfast love endures through all time.

> For God so loved the world, that he gave his only begotten Son, that whosoever believeth in him should not perish, but have everlasting life.
>
> —John 3:16

Sometimes, Father, you seem distant and unreal. My faith falters. When it does, please help me remember how much you love me. It wasn't just words, but actions: you sent your son Jesus to save me.

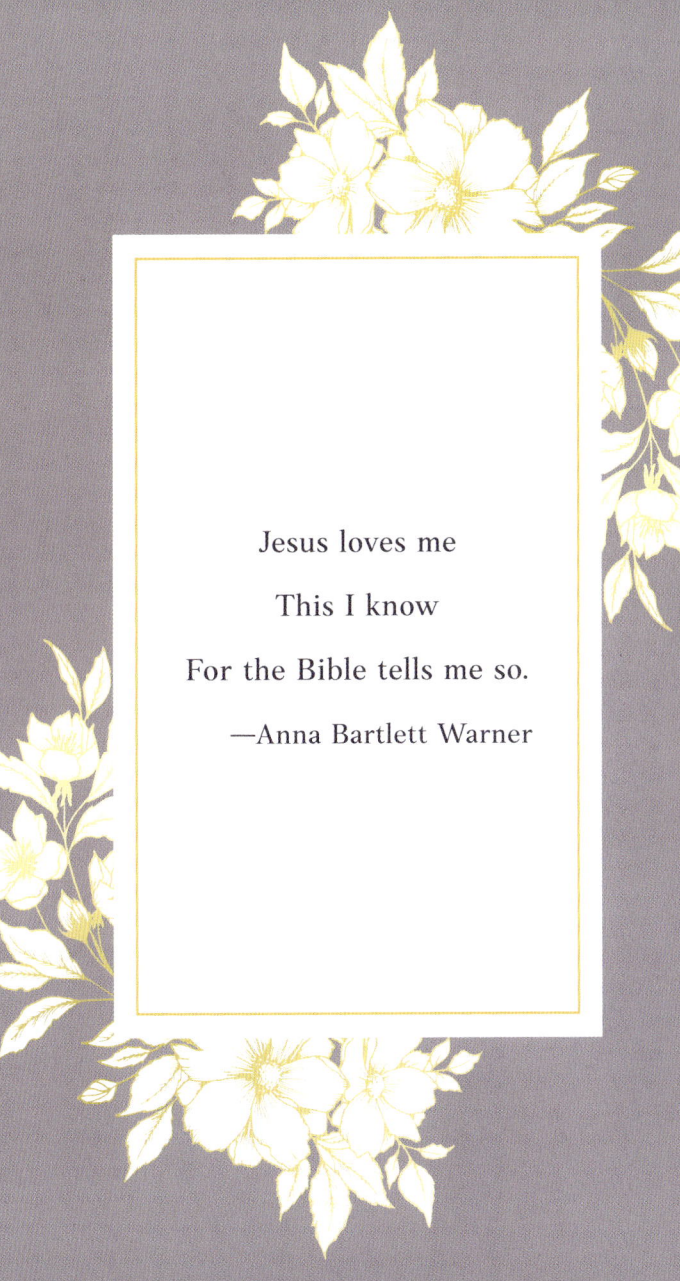

Jesus loves me

This I know

For the Bible tells me so.

—Anna Bartlett Warner

> I will worship toward thy holy temple, and praise thy name for thy lovingkindness and for thy truth: for thou hast magnified thy word above all thy name.
>
> —Psalm 138:2

God's awesome might and power can be intimidating, but we don't need to be afraid, for God looks at us with lovingkindness, seeing our flaws but forgiving us.

> The grace of the Lord Jesus Christ, and the love of God, and the communion of the Holy Ghost, be with you all.
>
> —2 Corinthians 13:14

This prayer of Paul's is a beautiful blessing that we can still use today, spreading the love of God to our family, friends, and community.

Deliver me, O God, from a slothful mind, from all lukewarmness, and all dejection of spirit. I know these cannot but deaden my love to you; mercifully free my heart from them, and give me a lively, zealous, active, and cheerful spirit, that I may vigorously perform whatever you command, thankfully suffer whatever you choose for me, and be ever ardent to obey in all things your holy love.

—John Wesley

For this cause I bow my knees unto the Father of our Lord Jesus Christ, Of whom the whole family in heaven and earth is named, That he would grant you, according to the riches of his glory, to be strengthened with might by his Spirit in the inner man; That Christ may dwell in your hearts by faith; that ye, being rooted and grounded in love, May be able to comprehend with all saints what is the breadth, and length, and depth, and height; And to know the love of Christ, which passeth knowledge, that ye might be filled with all the fulness of God.

—Ephesians 3:14–19

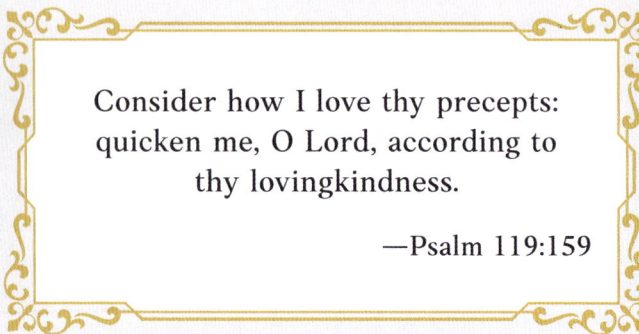

Consider how I love thy precepts: quicken me, O Lord, according to thy lovingkindness.

—Psalm 119:159

Other versions of the Bible translate "quicken me" as "revive me," "give me life," "cause me to live," and "make me live again." God's love gives us both physical and spiritual life. We are dependent on his love for our very existence.

> My love be with you all in Christ Jesus. Amen.
>
> —1 Corinthians 16:24

When we believe in God's love, when we trust and have confidence in it, we can spread it to others. Dear Jesus, please help me share your love with others in a way that draws them ultimately to you.

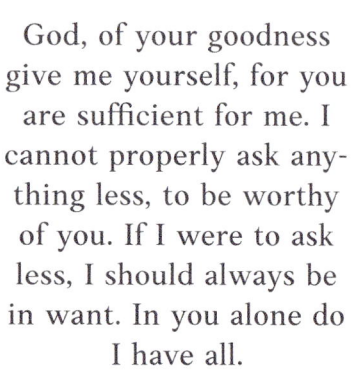

God, of your goodness give me yourself, for you are sufficient for me. I cannot properly ask anything less, to be worthy of you. If I were to ask less, I should always be in want. In you alone do I have all.

—Julian of Norwich

As the Father hath loved me, so have I loved you: continue ye in my love.

—John 15:9

God is love, and our love for God and each other is a reflection of that love between the Father and Son. God, please help me grow in love. Amen.

COMFORT AND HEALING

In my distress I cried unto the Lord,
and he heard me.

—Psalm 120:1

Whether my distress is physical, emotional, mental, or spiritual, I can cry to the Lord like the psalmist. Thank you, Lord, for this assurance that you hear me when I call to you.

Have we trials and temptations?

Is there trouble anywhere?

We should never be discouraged,

Take it to the Lord in prayer.

Can we find a friend so faithful

Who will all our sorrows share?

Jesus knows our every weakness,

Take it to the Lord in prayer.

—Joseph M. Scriven

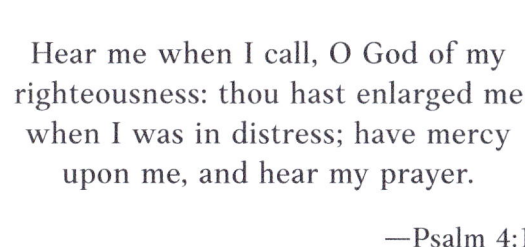

> Hear me when I call, O God of my righteousness: thou hast enlarged me when I was in distress; have mercy upon me, and hear my prayer.
>
> —Psalm 4:1

Lord, I don't know what to do. I'm having a disagreement with a longtime friend over an issue of morality. I generally respect this friend's ideas, but I think she's wrong here. I don't like the divisiveness between us, and I worry I'm being judgmental, but I also can't be dishonest about something I see as wrong. Please grant me wisdom in dealing with this. If I'm wrong, please give me clarity and correction. If I'm right, please help me find the right words and guide us both in interpreting your commandments and your will as we navigate this thorny issue.

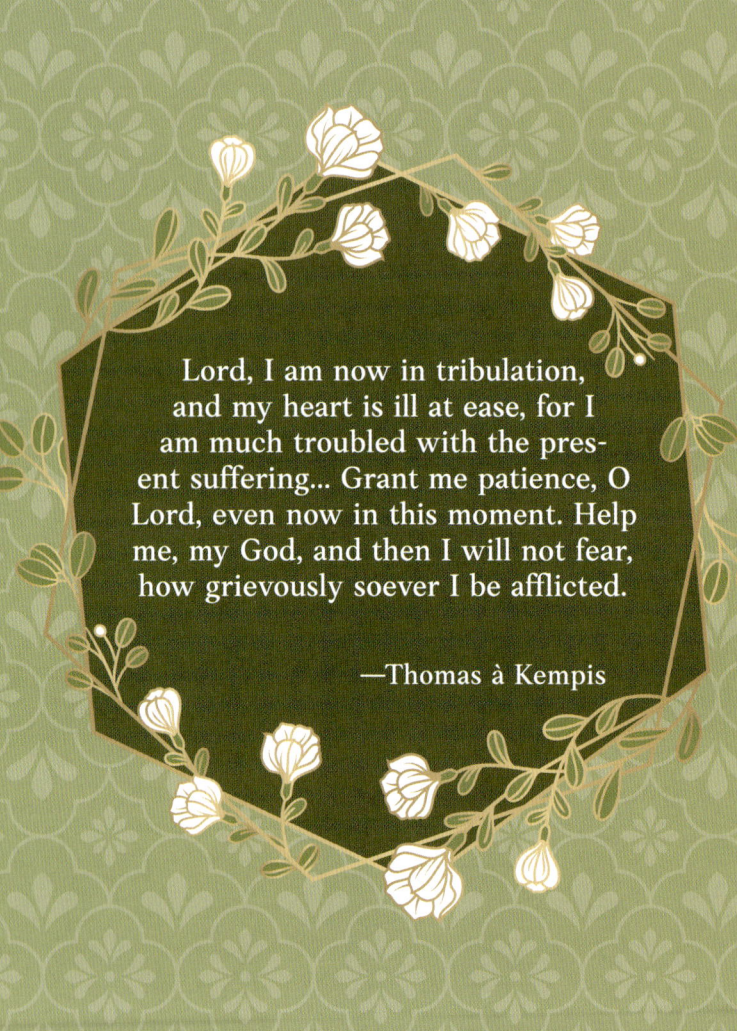

Lord, I am now in tribulation, and my heart is ill at ease, for I am much troubled with the present suffering... Grant me patience, O Lord, even now in this moment. Help me, my God, and then I will not fear, how grievously soever I be afflicted.

—Thomas à Kempis

In my distress I called upon the Lord, and cried unto my God: he heard my voice out of his temple, and my cry came before him, even into his ears.

—Psalm 18:6

O Lord, you know very well that when times get hard, I find it more difficult to go to church. It feels like an effort to drag myself out of bed. But today I did, and I found a measure of peace sitting there quietly. Please help me, Lord. Help me with my current crop of problems, and help me to remember to turn to you.

> Likewise the Spirit also helpeth our infirmities: for we know not what we should pray for as we ought: but the Spirit itself maketh intercession for us with groanings which cannot be uttered.
>
> —Romans 8:26

I don't know what to pray for in this situation. I'm at a loss for words, and I don't know whether to ask for healing or acceptance.

You know what's best, Lord. I turn everything over to you.

> The troubles of my heart are enlarged:
> O bring thou me out of my distresses.
>
> —Psalm 25:17

At work, we've been told impending layoffs are coming, right as my spouse is expecting an influx of medical bills. Even if I'm not one of those laid off, even if my family comes out of this fine, I worry about those colleagues who will be let go. The stress of this situation is making me lose sleep, God, and I know that's magnifying the problem. Please soothe my frantic mind and let me find peace in my heart, whatever comes.

> Then they cried unto the Lord in their trouble, and he delivered them out of their distresses.
>
> —Psalm 107:6

This verse shows up several times as a refrain in Psalm 107, as the psalmist talks about how God saved people in the past, like the people of Israel in the desert, and continues to save people in the present time, like sailors afflicted by storms at sea. God, grant me faith that you still work in this present age. Let me cry out to you as people have for generations, trusting in your goodness.

> And when Jesus departed thence, two blind men followed him, crying, and saying, Thou son of David, have mercy on us.
>
> —Matthew 9:27

I need physical healing, Lord. The arthritis is becoming increasingly painful, and it's stopping me from doing things. Like those who cried out to Jesus to heal their physical ailments, I call out to you now: have mercy on me.

> I called upon the Lord in distress:
> the Lord answered me, and set me in a large place.
>
> —Psalm 118:5

I come to you today in thanksgiving. My old job was toxic, and you helped me discern that it was time to leave. I'm at a new place now, and things seem promising. Thank you for leading me here. I ask that it continue to be a good match for me, a place where I can use and build my skills and talents.

> O sing unto the Lord a new song; for he hath done marvellous things: his right hand, and his holy arm, hath gotten him the victory.
>
> —Psalm 98:1

Lord, after a rough patch during his teenage years where my son was often moody and even mean, he is thriving at college. I'm so proud of him and how he's turned things around, and I rejoice in how we can talk more easily, without every topic becoming a minefield. Most of all, I rejoice in his present happiness. Thank you for your guidance during these last years!

O God, our help in ages past,

Our hope for years to come;

Bet thou our guide while life shall last,

And our eternal home.

Under the shadow of thy throne,

Still may we dwell secure;

Sufficient is thine arm alone,

And our defense is sure.

—Isaac Watts

The Lord also will be a refuge for the oppressed, a refuge in times of trouble.

—Psalm 9:9

I hold up in prayer today those who have had to flee their homes, driven away by natural disasters or regional strife. May you ease their burdens and give a heart of generosity to those they encounter as they return to rebuild or establish themselves in new homes.

I was sinking deep in sin,

Far from the peaceful shore,

Very deeply stained within,

Sinking to rise no more;

But the Master of the sea

Heard my despairing cry,

From the waters lifted me–

Now safe am I.

—James Rowe

> I will say unto God my rock,
> Why hast thou forgotten me?
> why go I mourning because of
> the oppression of the enemy?
>
> —Psalm 42:9

Lord, after a period of wondering whether I was imagining a chill in some friendships, I finally heard today that one woman in our group of friends has been spreading rumors about me. I'm so hurt and so angry. While we were never very close ourselves, I've been blindsided by this—I never would have expected it of her. It hurts even more that some of my closer friends apparently believed her lies without questioning them. I feel alienated from my friends and forgotten by you, and it hurts! Please give me faith that you're there for me after all, and guide me through this time.

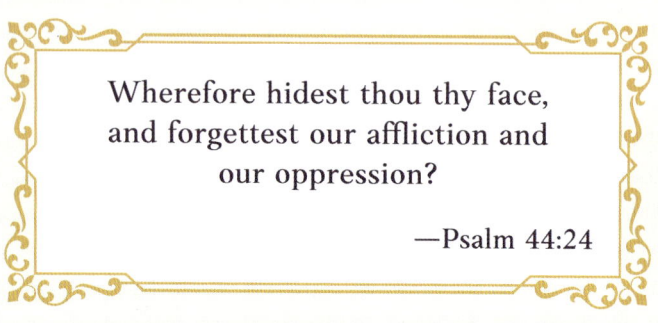

> Wherefore hidest thou thy face,
> and forgettest our affliction and
> our oppression?
>
> —Psalm 44:24

A friend used to say about problems, "Well, at least it's not cancer." That's stuck in my head over the years, but this time it is cancer. My instinctive feeling is to wonder how you could let this happen. I'm angry at the diagnosis, angry at the doctors, angry at you. I feel like I should be praying for peace and acceptance and healing, but I don't have words for that. Right now, I'm in this moment of anger, and that honest anger is what I bring to you now, hoping it won't last forever.

Dear God,

Drop thy still dews
of quietness,

Till all our strivings cease;

Take from our souls the
strain and stress,

And let our ordered lives
confess

Thy beauty of thy peace.

—John Greenleaf Whittier

> Be merciful unto me, O God: for man would swallow me up; he fighting daily oppresseth me.
>
> —Psalm 56:1

I've read the documents, filled in the forms, and spent my time going through the phone tree, but the insurance company keeps denying our claims. Please help me, Lord, in this struggle. Help me unlock the right combination of words and forms, or help me reach someone on the other side who will act with integrity in processing the claim properly.

But as for me, my prayer is unto thee, O Lord, in an acceptable time: O God, in the multitude of thy mercy hear me, in the truth of thy salvation. Deliver me out of the mire, and let me not sink: let me be delivered from them that hate me, and out of the deep waters.

—Psalm 69:13–14

> O let not the oppressed return ashamed: let the poor and needy praise thy name.
>
> —Psalm 74:21

Today I pray for the homeless, as well as those who suffer from housing insecurity. Please guide all who need it to new, safe homes, and protect them in the meantime.

There is no sorrow, Lord, too light

To bring in prayer to thee;

There is no anxious care too slight

To wake thy sympathy.

Thou, who hast trod the thorny road,

Wilt share each small distress;

The love which bore the greater load

Will not refuse the less.

There is no secret sigh we breathe

But meets thine ear divine;

And every cross grows light beneath,

The shadow, Lord of thine.

—Jane Crewdson

> Have mercy upon me, O Lord; for I am weak: O Lord, heal me; for my bones are vexed.
>
> —Psalm 6:2

It's just the flu, but it feels every muscle and bone in my body is aching. My head hurts and I'm beyond tired. Please help me get through this, and not just me, but everyone who's suffering from illness.

O Lord my God, I cried unto thee, and thou hast healed me.

—Psalm 30:2

Thank you, God! I've been so scared this past week while we waited for the results of the biopsy. I don't know if the initial tests that showed something potentially wrong were just a false alarm or if you healed me, but either way, I'm grateful. Praise you, God!

Pass me not, O gentle Savior,

Hear my humble cry,

While on others thou art calling,

Do not pass me by.

Savior, Savior,

Hear my humble cry;

While on others thou art calling,

Do not pass me by.

—Fanny Crosby

> He healeth the broken in heart, and bindeth up their wounds.
>
> —Psalm 147:3

How can this be possible, Lord? One day I would have said I was in a basically happy marriage—that we had problems, sure, but nothing insurmountable. The next day, my husband was leaving, saying he'd fallen in love with someone else, and he didn't want to try to rescue our marriage. I'm heartbroken.

Please be my comfort during these times. Please give me strength in helping the kids deal with this abrupt change in their lives. Please help me as I make the change from wife to co-parent, that my actions and words not be tainted by bitterness. When all else is dissolving, I turn to you, my rock.

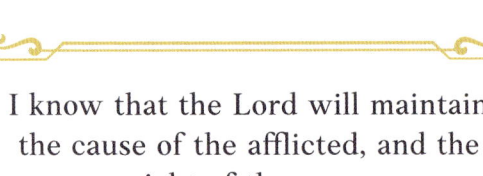

> I know that the Lord will maintain the cause of the afflicted, and the right of the poor.
>
> —Psalm 140:12

Please help all those who are in the hospital today, Lord. Let those who are going in for tests, those who are recovering, and those who are dying feel your presence with them. Instill strength in those getting a life-changing diagnosis. Comfort those who are in waiting rooms, hoping for positive news of their loved ones. And hearten the medical, janitorial, and administrative staff who are doing their best for patients.

Many are the afflictions of the righteous: but the Lord delivereth him out of them all.

—Psalm 34:19

A friend from church is going through a difficult time, Lord: her husband just lost his job, she's having a flareup of some chronic health issues, and someone sideswiped their car in a parking lot. She has a strong, sustaining faith, but I know she's beginning to feel discouraged. Please help her during these times. Amen.

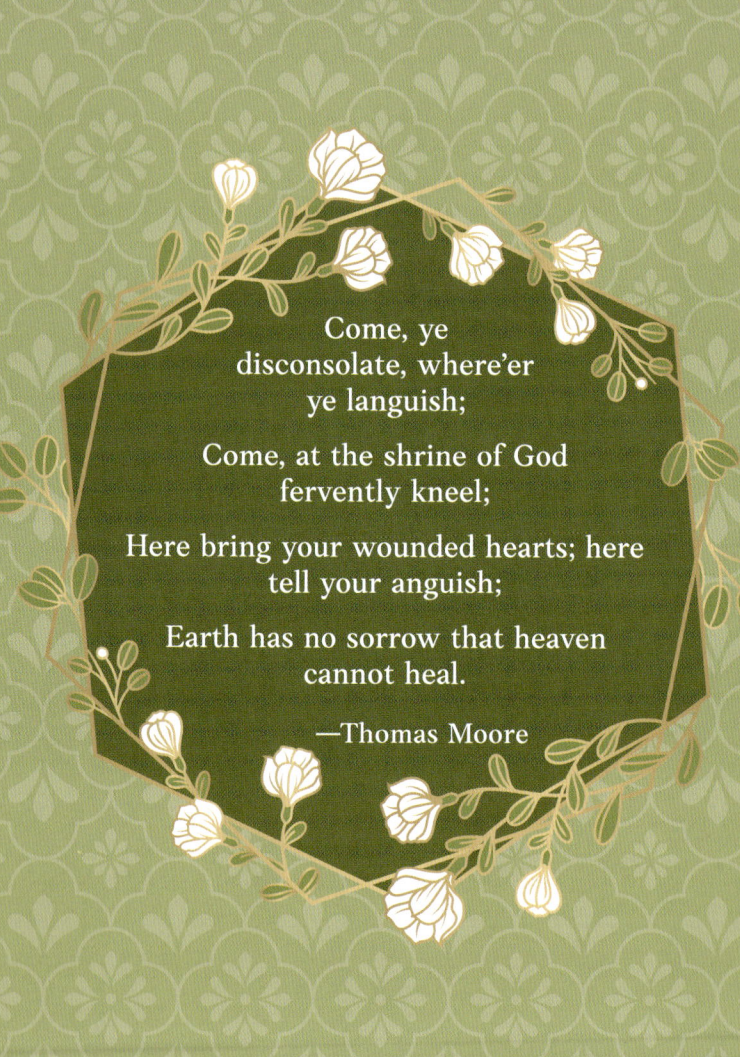

Come, ye disconsolate, where'er ye languish;

Come, at the shrine of God fervently kneel;

Here bring your wounded hearts; here tell your anguish;

Earth has no sorrow that heaven cannot heal.

—Thomas Moore

This is my comfort in my affliction: for thy word hath quickened me.

—Psalm 119:50

My grandma was a woman of prayer. I remember her sitting with her Bible, reading the Psalms, while we were sitting vigil during my grandfather's last days. Thank you, Lord, for the comfort you provided her, and the reminder of the value of your Word.

The sorrows of death compassed me.

—Psalm 18:4

Lord, I am grieving. I don't know how to bear this loss. Please be with me now.

Heal us, Emmanuel, hear our prayer; we wait to feel thy touch; deep-wounded souls to thee repair, and Savior, we are such.

—William Cowper

For I am ready to halt, and my sorrow is continually before me.

—Psalm 38:17

I'm so tired. Caregiving for my aging dad as he declines is so hard. I cling to the moments we have of love and lucidity, even as I see him slide further into dementia. His body is healthy even as his mind deteriorates: I don't see an end to this. God, I don't know what to do. I ask simply for your presence today.

There is a balm in Gilead

To make the wounded whole,

There is a balm in Gilead

To heal the sin-sick soul.

Sometimes I feel discouraged

And think my work's in vain,

But then the Holy Spirit

Revives my soul again.

—Traditional

> But I am poor and sorrowful: let thy salvation, O God, set me up on high.
>
> —Psalm 69:29

I'm worried about the household finances, Lord. With that last set of unexpected expenses, we've run through more of our savings than I'd like. I don't like the uncertainty of living paycheck to paycheck, praying that there won't be a disaster that tips us over the edge. Please help me remember to trust you, Lord, to give us our daily bread.

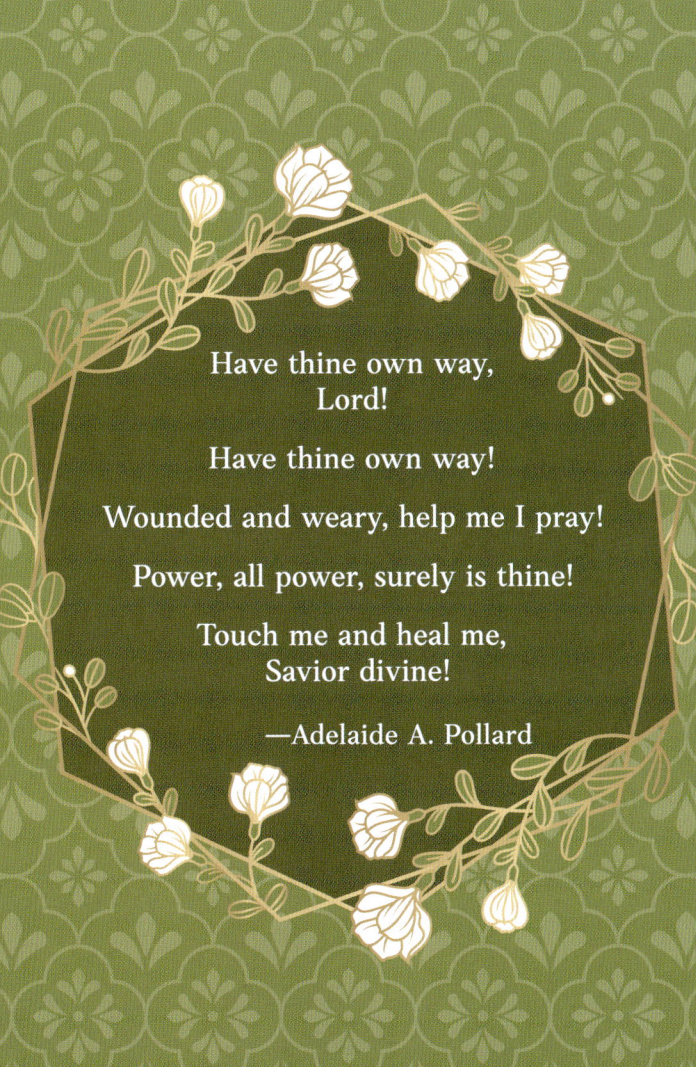

Have thine own way,
Lord!

Have thine own way!

Wounded and weary, help me I pray!

Power, all power, surely is thine!

Touch me and heal me,
Savior divine!

—Adelaide A. Pollard

The sorrows of death compassed me,
and the pains of hell gat hold upon me:
I found trouble and sorrow.

—Psalm 116:3

Lord, I don't know what the outcome of this surgery will be. The risks are high, but so is the risk of doing nothing. Please be with me today. Please be with my family as they wait, and if something happens to me. I'm scared, even as I try to let go and put this matter in your hands.

Blessed is he that considereth the poor: the Lord will deliver him in time of trouble. The Lord will preserve him, and keep him alive; and he shall be blessed upon the earth: and thou wilt not deliver him unto the will of his enemies. The Lord will strengthen him upon the bed of languishing: thou wilt make all his bed in his sickness.

—Psalm 41:1–3

> It is vain for you to rise up early,
> to sit up late, to eat the bread
> of sorrows: for so he giveth his
> beloved sleep.
>
> —Psalm 127:2

God, I have not been sleeping well. One daughter is having issues in her marriage; the other is still having neck and back issues from a car accident. My husband's mother is growing forgetful, in a way that might just be part of aging but might be something worse. My own parents are struggling in their home but don't want to downsize.

But what good does it do anyone, for me to toss and turn at night, brooding and worrying? I turn these problems over to you, Lord.

Heal me, O Lord, and I shall be healed; save me, and I shall be saved: for thou art my praise.

—Jeremiah 17:14

Chronic pain is no joke, God. It fluctuates, but I'm finding it harder to remember a time I wasn't in pain. I ask for your healing and strength.

I cried unto God with my voice, even unto God with my voice; and he gave ear unto me. In the day of my trouble I sought the Lord: my sore ran in the night, and ceased not: my soul refused to be comforted. I remembered God, and was troubled: I complained, and my spirit was overwhelmed. Selah.

Thou holdest mine eyes waking: I am so troubled that I cannot speak. I have considered the days of old, the years of ancient times. I call to remembrance my song in the night: I commune with mine own heart: and my spirit made diligent search. Will the Lord cast off for ever? and will he be favourable no more? Is his mercy clean gone for ever? doth his promise fail for evermore? Hath God forgotten to be gracious? hath he in anger shut up his tender mercies? Selah.

And I said, This is my infirmity: but I will remember the years of the right hand of the most High. I will remember the works of the Lord: surely I will remember thy wonders of old. I will meditate also of all thy work, and talk of thy doings. Thy way, O God, is in the sanctuary: who is so great a God as our God? Thou art the God that doest wonders: thou hast declared thy strength among the people. Thou hast with thine arm redeemed thy people, the sons of Jacob and Joseph. Selah.

The waters saw thee, O God, the waters saw thee; they were afraid: the depths also were troubled. The clouds poured out water: the skies sent out a sound: thine arrows also went abroad. The voice of thy thunder was in the heaven: the lightnings lightened the world: the earth trembled and shook. Thy way is in the sea, and thy path in the great waters, and thy footsteps are not known. Thou leddest thy people like a flock by the hand of Moses and Aaron.

—Psalm 77

And when Jesus was entered into Capernaum, there came unto him a centurion, beseeching him, And saying, Lord, my servant lieth at home sick of the palsy, grievously tormented. And Jesus saith unto him, I will come and heal him. The centurion answered and said, Lord, I am not worthy that thou shouldest come under my roof: but speak the word only, and my servant shall be healed.

—Matthew 8:5–8

Like the centurion, I pray for the health of someone I love, in this case my oldest friend. Speak the word, and she will be healed.

> Let, I pray thee, thy merciful kindness be for my comfort, according to thy word unto thy servant.
>
> —Psalm 119:76

I'm homesick, Lord, for my old home. I know the move was the right decision, and I'm glad to live in an era of texts and e-mails that make communication easy, but tonight I'm feeling lonely and I miss seeing my old neighbors and friends in person. I ask for your comfort now.

Where there is charity and wisdom,

there is neither fear nor ignorance.

Where there is patience and humility,

there is neither anger nor vexation.

Where there is poverty and joy,

there is neither greed nor avarice.

Where there is peace and meditation,

there is neither anxiety nor doubt.

—St. Francis of Assisi

Bless the Lord, O my soul: and all that is within me, bless his holy name. Bless the Lord, O my soul, and forget not all his benefits: Who forgiveth all thine iniquities; who healeth all thy diseases; Who redeemeth thy life from destruction; who crowneth thee with lovingkindness and tender mercies; Who satisfieth thy mouth with good things; so that thy youth is renewed like the eagle's.

—Psalm 103:1–5

TRUST

O taste and see that the Lord is
good: blessed is the man
that trusteth in him.

—Psalm 34:8

I don't always see you working in my life, until afterward, when I look back at some event or time period and realize, "Ah, that happened in just the right way." You do good things for me, Lord, and I am so grateful!

'Tis so sweet to trust
in Jesus,

And to take him at
his word;

Just to rest upon
his promise,

And to know, "Thus saith
the Lord."

Jesus, Jesus, how I
trust him!

How I've proved him o'er
and o'er!

Jesus, Jesus, precious
Jesus!

O for grace to trust him
more!

—Louisa M. R. Stead

> For thou wilt light my candle: the Lord my God will enlighten my darkness.
>
> —Psalm 18:28

Help me remember that you won't always give me all the answers I want at once. Every day, I need to put my trust in you again, believing that you will give me a candle's worth of light—enough to see my next step, if not the full journey ahead of me. In the Lord's Prayer, we ask for our "daily bread," knowing that each day, we need to trust that you will nourish us. Lord, I ask for a little bit of light today into the problem I've been wrestling with—enough insight to sustain me.

For thou art my hope, O Lord God: thou art my trust from my youth.

—Psalm 71:5

Lord, please give me the simple faith of a child who trusts that her parents know everything and can do anything. You, my heavenly Father, are deserving of that faith and trust!

Trust not in oppression, and become not vain in robbery: if riches increase, set not your heart upon them.

—Psalm 62:10

Lord, please lead me on the path of righteousness. Let me not set myself above others, or equate wealth and worldly success with godliness.

O God, from whom to be turned is to fall,

To whom to be turned is to rise,

And with whom to stand is to abide for ever;

Grant us in all our duties your help,

In all our perplexities your guidance,

In all our dangers your protection,

And in all our sorrows your peace,

Through Jesus Christ our Lord, Amen.

—St. Augustine

> Trust in the Lord, and do good; so shalt thou dwell in the land, and verily thou shalt be fed.
>
> —Psalm 37:3

Lord, how often we get bogged down in the "what-ifs" of an opportunity instead of trusting you and moving forward. Teach us to look at the big picture, Lord—to catch the vision of what you want to accomplish through us. Then give us the courage to move forward in faith, knowing that you will be with us.

He shall not be afraid of evil tidings: his heart is fixed, trusting in the Lord.

—Psalm 112:7

Father, newspaper headlines remind us continually of tragic accidents to children in their own homes. You are our shield against danger. We put our trust in you. We thank you for the protection you have already provided, and we depend on your help in making our home a safe place for our children.

Guard us from carelessness, and heighten our awareness of dangerous situations that need to be corrected. Help us to find ways to protect our children, and prevent us from thoughtlessly putting them at risk.

Heavenly Father, you love our children as we do, and we cling to your promise that they will dwell in safety with you as their protector.

Some trust in chariots, and some in horses: but we will remember the name of the Lord our God.

—Psalm 20:7

Things break, fall apart, and decay. Cars break down, jobs are lost, and even our bodies can betray us. By contrast, God never fails.

My times are in thy hand;

My God, I wish them there;

My life, my friends, my soul I leave

Entirely to thy care.

—William F. Lloyd

> O Lord my God, in thee do I put my trust: save me from all them that persecute me, and deliver me: Lest he tear my soul like a lion, rending it in pieces, while there is none to deliver.
>
> —Psalm 7:1–2

I think it's good for me to be able to see my frustrations, difficulties, and sorrows as "proving grounds" for my growing trust in you, Lord. From difficulty finding fulfilling work to bills I'm struggling to pay to a disagreement with a loved one, life brings every kind of opportunity for me to look to you for help. Today is a great day to choose to not get wrapped around my own axle when I'm faced with frustrations and fears. I'm putting all of the "proving ground" stuff I'm facing right now into your hands, and I trust you with the outcome.

Be merciful unto me, O God, be merciful unto me: for my soul trusteth in thee: yea, in the shadow of thy wings will I make my refuge, until these calamities be overpast.

—Psalm 57:1

I'm stressed out, but I sit and breathe peacefully, and imagine the shadow of your wings covering me like a blanket. I envision your love wrapping around me and surrounding me, keeping me safe and whole.

It is better to trust in the Lord than to put confidence in man. It is better to trust in the Lord than to put confidence in princes.

—Psalm 118:8–9

It's hard when someone in a position of authority—whether it be a pastor, a political figure, or the head of our local PTA—does something disappointing. But people inevitably falter. Please help me forgive the stumbling of our leaders while still standing up for your values, remembering that you never fail.

> But I trusted in thee, O Lord: I said, Thou art my God.
>
> —Psalm 31:14

Lord, I know that doubts and confusion don't come from you. On days when everything I know to be true is challenged—and I feel like I'm walking through a fog that won't lift—be my source of truth and light. Bring me back to complete trust in you.

Trust in him at all times; ye people, pour out your heart before him: God is a refuge for us.

—Psalm 62:8

Cast away your anxieties and place your trust in the Lord.

Before me peaceful,

Behind me peaceful,

Under me peaceful,

Over me peaceful,

All around me peaceful.

—Traditional

Our fathers trusted in thee: they trusted, and thou didst deliver them.

—Psalm 22:4

I miss my parents, God. They were people of faith, and well into adulthood, I knew that if I expressed some concern to them, they would take it to God in prayer. I wish I could pray about my current problems with them, though I am grateful that they modeled an active prayer life for me. Like them, I turn to you now, trusting that you will listen.

Simply trusting every day,

Trusting through a stormy way;

Even when my faith is small,

Trusting Jesus, that is all.

Trusting as the moments fly,

Trusting as the days go by;

Trusting him whate'er befall,

Trusting Jesus, that is all.

—Edgar Page

> For I will not trust in my bow,
> neither shall my sword save me.
>
> —Psalm 44:6

I can take reasonable precautions to keep myself safe and healthy—lock my doors, get a physical every year—but I don't have ultimate control. I might suffer from a car accident or a health problem or a natural disaster. God, I place my life in your hands, trusting that you will be with me through whatever problems life brings.

And they that know thy name will put their trust in thee: for thou, Lord, hast not forsaken them that seek thee.

—Psalm 9:10

God, thank you for the women in my prayer group. They are an inspiration to me! Seeing their trust and faith helps bolster my own. I hope that my faith can be an example to them too!

I will trust in the Lord,

I will trust in the Lord,

I will trust in the Lord till I die.

I will trust in the Lord,

I will trust in the Lord,

I will trust in the Lord till I die.

—Traditional spiritual

O my God, I trust in thee: let me not be ashamed, let not mine enemies triumph over me.

—Psalm 25:2

Lord, I'm giving a small speech at my Bible study, and I am so nervous. Today, my enemy is my own self-doubt. I ask you for confidence. I ask you for a voice that does not falter. I ask you for inspiration and guidance, that my thoughts, words, and plans be aligned with yours. Amen.

> Blessed is that man that maketh the Lord his trust, and respecteth not the proud, nor such as turn aside to lies.
>
> —Psalm 40:4

One of my neighbors is charismatic and charming, the "queen bee" of the community. She can be a little manipulative about getting her way, and I find myself wanting to stay on her good side. I know the dynamic isn't fully healthy—part of me feels like I'm back in middle school, trying to get in with the popular kids! Please help me get some emotional detachment from this situation and stay true to myself.

When we walk with
the Lord

In the light of his word,

What a glory he sheds
on our way!

While we do his
good will,

He abides with us still,

And with all who will
trust and obey.

—John H. Sammis

In thee, O Lord, do I put my trust: let me never be put to confusion.

—Psalm 71:1

Lord, a vexing situation has me very confused. Is it possible I'm trying to sort it out through my own limited understanding and overlooking a crucial element? I know I can trust you with anything. I give this up to you and ask you to restore me to a place where I can look at what's going on in the right way—your way.

> The Lord is my strength and my shield; my heart trusted in him, and I am helped: therefore my heart greatly rejoiceth; and with my song will I praise him.
>
> —Psalm 28:7

Thank you, thank you, thank you! I had to have a tricky conversation with my adult daughter regarding some things I've observed about how her current boyfriend treats her. Now that she's grown up, it can be hard to know when to wait for my daughter to bring something up, when to speak regardless, when to give advice, and when just to listen. I haven't wanted to overstep and cause my daughter to dismiss my concerns, so I've been praying to God to provide an opportunity to speak and the right words, and today we had a hard but good conversation. I am so grateful!

> In the Lord put I my trust: how say ye to my soul, Flee as a bird to your mountain?
>
> —Psalm 11:1

Today has been daunting. Everything feels like it's going wrong. I retreat to my bedroom at the end of the day, curl up on the bed with blankets and my Bible, and turn to you, my rest and my refuge.

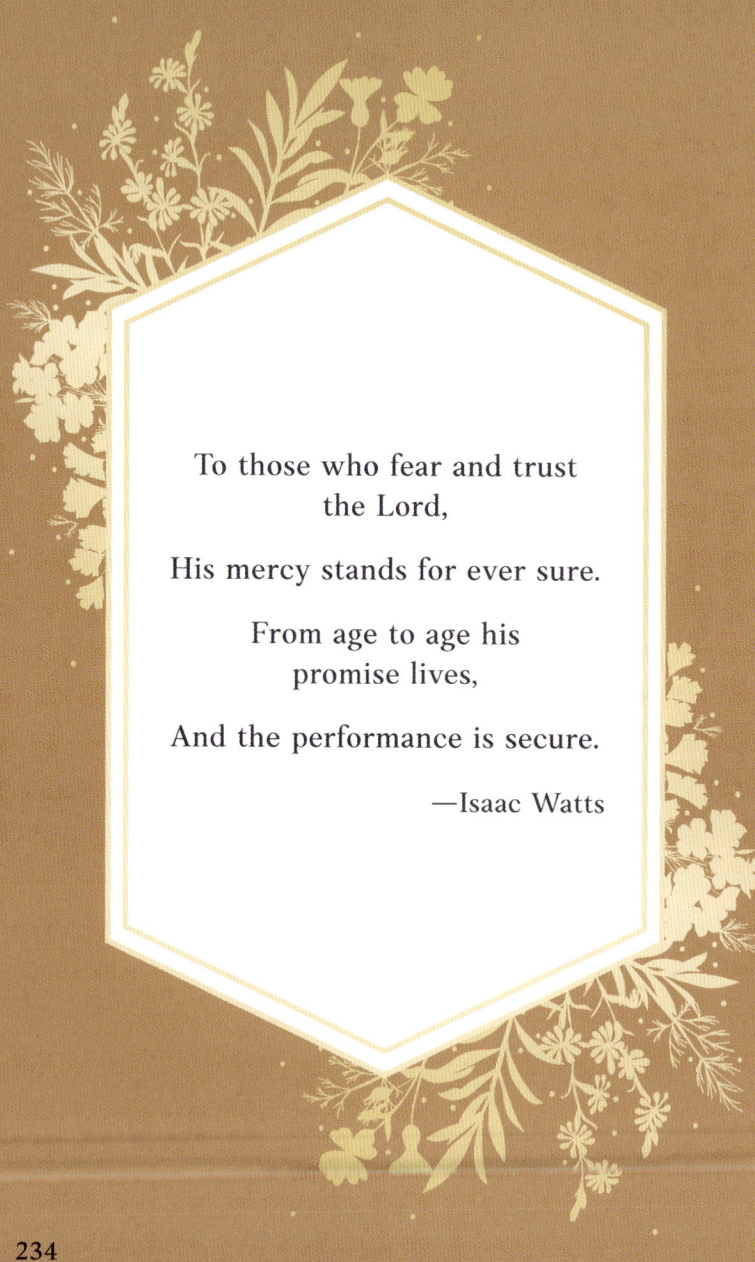

To those who fear and trust
the Lord,

His mercy stands for ever sure.

From age to age his
promise lives,

And the performance is secure.

—Isaac Watts

But I am like a green olive tree in the house of God: I trust in the mercy of God for ever and ever.

—Psalm 52:8

When I was young I thought the adults knew everything. As an adult, I know how wrong I was! I'm still growing and learning, Lord. Growing in faith, growing in love, growing in trust, growing in hope. Thank you, Lord, for the gift of growth.

> Judge me, O Lord; for I have walked in mine integrity: I have trusted also in the Lord; therefore I shall not slide.
>
> —Psalm 26:1

Judgment can be a scary word. The psalmist, though, is unafraid. Dear Lord, let me have such integrity and trust that I do not fear your judgment.

Come, every soul by sin oppressed,

There's mercy with the Lord;

And he will surely give you rest,

By trusting in his word.

Only trust him, only trust him,

Only trust him now;

He will save you,

He will save you,

He will save you now.

—John H. Stockton

Preserve me, O God: for in thee do I put my trust.

—Psalm 16:1

There are few things scarier about aging than moments of forgetfulness. So often when I forget something, I wonder if this is normal forgetfulness like anyone might experience, a standard part of aging, or the precursor to something worse. Having seen my own mom and grandmother struggle with dementia, I fear it. I ask that you spare me that fate, Lord, though ultimately thy will, not mine, be done.

In God I will praise his word, in God I have put my trust; I will not fear what flesh can do unto me.

—Psalm 56:4

I have to talk to the doctor about some ominous symptoms. It might be nothing—I hope it is! But after some Internet research, I am worried about worst-case scenarios. Please help me navigate this period of uncertainty and anxiety, Lord, until I have answers.

On Christ, the solid Rock, I stand:

All other ground is sinking sand;

All other ground is sinking sand.

—Edward Mote

> Oh how great is thy goodness, which thou hast laid up for them that fear thee; which thou hast wrought for them that trust in thee before the sons of men!
>
> —Psalm 31:19

Thank you for good pastors, Lord! Thank you for those who radiate your love as they do the work of helping the rest of us along our spiritual journeys. They're a blessing to us; may they be blessed in turn with your great goodness.

The Lord is my rock, and my fortress, and my deliverer; my God, my strength, in whom I will trust; my buckler, and the horn of my salvation, and my high tower.

—Psalm 18:2

I looked it up once, and a buckler is a type of shield. When I am feeling battered by the animosity of others, Lord, you are my shield. Thank you for your protection.

How excellent is thy lovingkindness, O God! therefore the children of men put their trust under the shadow of thy wings.

—Psalm 36:7

Lord Jesus, the dimensions of your love are hard for me to comprehend because there is no other love like yours. No human love can compare with how deeply and thoroughly you love me. But just trusting that there is such a love as yours is the perfect beginning point for an adventure of becoming delightfully lost in its immensity.

If you but trust in God to guide you

And place your confidence in him,

You'll find him always there beside you

To give you hope and strength within;

For those who trust God's changeless love

Build on the rock that will not move.

—Georg Neumark, trans. Catherine Winkworth

> But it is good for me to draw near to God: I have put my trust in the Lord God, that I may declare all thy works.
>
> —Psalm 73:28

A few weeks ago when I was walking with a newer friend, I brought up how my faith helped sustain me during a recent difficult period as my husband looked for a new job. Faith wasn't something we'd discussed much in depth before, and I did wonder later how she took it. Today, she reached out and asked for prayers, and I feel like our friendship has reached a deeper level.

Thank you, God, for those blessings that come of declaring your works!

For our heart shall rejoice in him, because we have trusted in his holy name.

—Psalm 33:21

Lord, how unworthy we feel of your son's prayers on our behalf, but how grateful we are for his intercession! It's all more marvelous, more mysterious than we can grasp, but because we trust your Word and your heart, we humbly thank him for caring so much about us. Surely his prayers are heard above all others!

He that dwelleth in the secret place of the most High shall abide under the shadow of the Almighty. I will say of the Lord, He is my refuge and my fortress: my God; in him will I trust. Surely he shall deliver thee from the snare of the fowler, and from the noisome pestilence. He shall cover thee with his feathers, and under his wings shalt thou trust: his truth shall be thy shield and buckler.

—Psalm 91:1–4

O Lord of hosts, blessed is the man
that trusteth in thee.

—Psalm 84:12

I want to let go and let God—I'm just not always good at doing so. Please help me increase my trust in you!

I am trusting you, Lord Jesus,

Trusting only you;

Trusting you for full salvation,

Free and true.

—Frances Ridley Havergal

> The Lord redeemeth the soul of his servants: and none of them that trust in him shall be desolate.
>
> —Psalm 34:22

Lord, sometimes I am overwhelmed when I see all the suffering in this world. I feel like I am flailing in a treacherous sea with no power to be of any assistance to anyone else. Through prayer I regain my senses, and I know it's not up to me to meet all the needs in the world. Please show me which assignments belong to me; help me to focus on those and trust that you are working on the others.

> What time I am afraid, I
> will trust in thee.
>
> —Psalm 56:3

It's late at night, and still there is much to do. Yet there is peace, holding on to a childlike trust that God is an ever-present companion, showing us how not to worry needlessly, burning the candle at both ends.

PRAISE

Praise ye the Lord. Praise God in his sanctuary: praise him in the firmament of his power. Praise him for his mighty acts: praise him according to his excellent greatness. Praise him with the sound of the trumpet: praise him with the psaltery and harp. Praise him with the timbrel and dance: praise him with stringed instruments and organs. Praise him upon the loud cymbals: praise him upon the high sounding cymbals. Let every thing that hath breath praise the Lord. Praise ye the Lord.

—Psalm 150

> Be thou exalted, Lord, in thine own strength: so will we sing and praise thy power.
>
> —Psalm 21:13

You are so powerful, Father God, and also so loving. How marvelous that you show us both strength and tenderness. We praise you for your strength and power as seen in the sweep of creation.

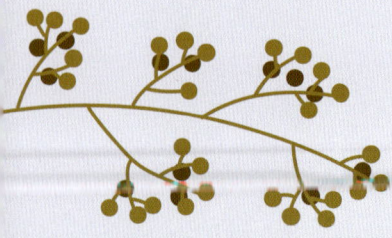

> This shall be written for the generation to come: and the people which shall be created shall praise the Lord.
>
> —Psalm 102:18

My husband and I set aside time each day for family prayer. Sometimes the kids drag their feet and mumble their words. But when it comes to praising you in song, they light up. Please let their pleasure in singing lead them to a deeper appreciation of prayer and of you.

Holy Spirit, the life that gives life.

You are the cause of all movement;

You are the breath of all creatures;

You are the salve that purifies
our souls;

You are the ointment that heals
our wounds;

You are the fire that warms
our hearts;

You are the light that guides
our feet.

Let all the world praise you.

—Hildegard of Bingen

Give unto the Lord, O ye mighty, give unto the Lord glory and strength. Give unto the Lord the glory due unto his name; worship the Lord in the beauty of holiness. The voice of the Lord is upon the waters: the God of glory thundereth: the Lord is upon many waters. The voice of the Lord is powerful; the voice of the Lord is full of majesty.

—Psalm 29:1–4

We're here at the ocean on vacation, and the immensity of the waves crashing reminds me of your power. You created both massive whales and the delicate creatures of tide pools, and I celebrate your might and majesty.

> Sing unto the Lord, praise ye the Lord: for he hath delivered the soul of the poor from the hand of evildoers.
>
> —Jeremiah 20:13

I'm worrying about so many things right now, Lord, especially my finances. While it's important to turn these concerns over to you in prayer, let me also remember to praise you, so that my prayer life isn't just a constant litany of complaints and requests. You're not a vending machine, Lord, but a person; please help me remember to extend my appreciation to you even during difficult times.

I will freely sacrifice unto thee:
I will praise thy name, O Lord;
for it is good.

—Psalm 54:6

I don't offer a sacrifice of burnt offerings, God, but of time. My time is really yours, of course—this lifetime that you have granted me—but I make the choice to turn that time back to you, seated in prayer, praising your name.

> I will praise thee, O Lord, with my whole heart; I will shew forth all thy marvellous works. I will be glad and rejoice in thee: I will sing praise to thy name, O thou most High.
>
> —Psalm 9:1–2

When I'm talking to friends, I want to praise you wholeheartedly, Lord, holding nothing back out of skepticism or fear of being seen as weird. I want to acknowledge your wonderful works in my life, bold and unafraid.

And David spake unto the Lord the words of this song in the day that the Lord had delivered him out of the hand of all his enemies, and out of the hand of Saul: And he said, The Lord is my rock, and my fortress, and my deliverer; The God of my rock; in him will I trust: he is my shield, and the horn of my salvation, my high tower, and my refuge, my saviour; thou savest me from violence. I will call on the Lord, who is worthy to be praised: so shall I be saved from mine enemies.

—2 Samuel 22:1–4

> Blessed and praised be the Lord, from whom comes all the good that we speak and think and do.
>
> —Teresa of Avila

Our source of goodness and life is you, Lord. I could not hug my children, read books, or dance with my husband if it were not for you. Thank you and praise you, Lord.

By him therefore let us offer the sacrifice of praise to God continually, that is, the fruit of our lips giving thanks to his name.

—Hebrews 13:15

Let me praise you, Lord, not just occasionally but every day, morning, noon, and night.

We will not hide them from their children, shewing to the generation to come the praises of the Lord, and his strength, and his wonderful works that he hath done.

—Psalm 78:4

My son is hitting his teenage years, and he's testing limits. As much as I know that's natural at this stage, and I want to give him room to spread his wings, I worry when his independence leads him to question or rebel against our family's faith and values. Please guide him during this time, God. And when this phase is said and done, let him see you as the source of all goodness and praise your name.

> Thy vows are upon me, O God: I will render praises unto thee.
>
> —Psalm 56:12

As I age, words don't always come as easily to me as they once did. It even shows up in my prayer life, Lord. But even if my words sometimes falter, I offer them to you with a sincere heart.

> In God will I praise his word: in the Lord will I praise his word.
>
> —Psalm 56:10

I praise your Word, God! I praise you for the guidance you have given us through scripture. I am grateful that through scripture, we can learn of and respond to your love.

By the word of the Lord were the heavens made; and all the host of them by the breath of his mouth.

—Psalm 33:6

We went to one of the national parks last summer, and the kids' mouths dropped in awe at seeing the array of stars in a truly dark sky. Those stars are a testament to your power and creativity, Lord. All things that you created give praise to you.

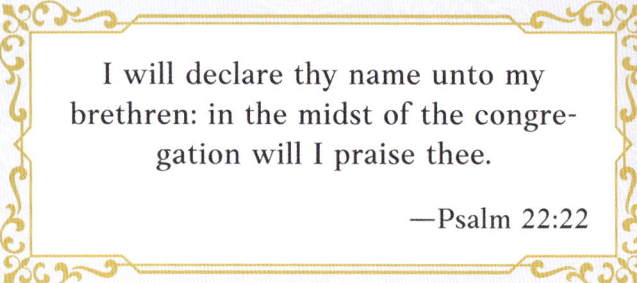

I will declare thy name unto my brethren: in the midst of the congregation will I praise thee.

—Psalm 22:22

It's a joy to sing at church with the rest of the congregation. Together, our voices soar to the heavens. We don't all have trained voices, but we hope our song pleases you.

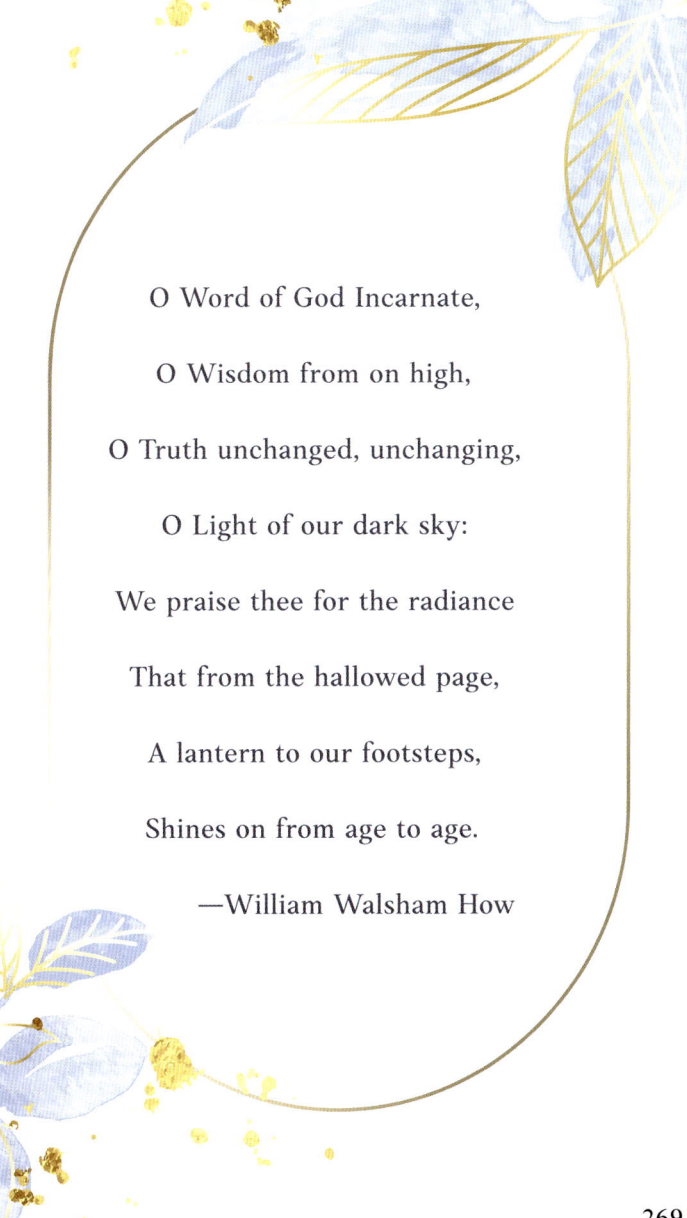

O Word of God Incarnate,

O Wisdom from on high,

O Truth unchanged, unchanging,

O Light of our dark sky:

We praise thee for the radiance

That from the hallowed page,

A lantern to our footsteps,

Shines on from age to age.

—William Walsham How

Bless the Lord, O my soul. O Lord my God, thou art very great; thou art clothed with honour and majesty. Who coverest thyself with light as with a garment: who stretchest out the heavens like a curtain: Who layeth the beams of his chambers in the waters: who maketh the clouds his chariot: who walketh upon the wings of the wind: Who maketh his angels spirits; his ministers a flaming fire: Who laid the foundations of the earth, that it should not be removed for ever.

—Psalm 104:1–5

> I will praise the Lord according to his righteousness: and will sing praise to the name of the Lord most high.
>
> —Psalm 7:17

You're so good, Father. You shower us with the blessings of life, love, family, and friends. You gave your son to save us. You love and forgive us. We praise your name.

> Make a joyful noise unto the Lord, all the earth: make a loud noise, and rejoice, and sing praise.
>
> —Psalm 98:4

The kids woke up early this morning and decided to form a band. I can't say it was the most peaceful awakening, or that my first reaction was pleasure, but their joy in singing was infectious. Thank you for their joyful noise.

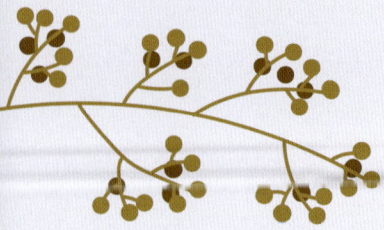

God is gone up with a shout, the Lord with the sound of a trumpet. Sing praises to God, sing praises: sing praises unto our King, sing praises. For God is the King of all the earth: sing ye praises with understanding. God reigneth over the heathen: God sitteth upon the throne of his holiness.

—Psalm 47:5–8

You're ultimately in charge, God. Our leaders may lead us astray or put in place policies that affect our lives negatively, but you do not fail us. Praise you, King and Leader of the world.

O Lord, thou art my God; I will exalt thee, I will praise thy name; for thou hast done wonderful things; thy counsels of old are faithfulness and truth.

—Isaiah 25:1

My parents were people of faith, but at some point I had to make the decision to continue to practice that faith as an adult. I had to consciously choose to say, like Isaiah, "Thou art my God." There have been times of struggles and doubt, but I choose to say it still. You are my God.

Oh that men
would praise the Lord for his
goodness, and for his wonderful
works to the children of men!

—Psalm 107:8

I'm meeting with some friends later today, as one of them has been going through a rough time and we want to support her. Along with listening, we'll likely pray for her in her distress. This verse inspires me to add some praise to our prayer session. We can together remember your goodness.

Let them praise thy great and terrible name; for it is holy.

—Psalm 99:3

Lord, sometimes I want faith on my own terms. I don't want to surrender to you completely or change my life or my behavior too much. Let me not try to set limits on your love and your work in my life, but just praise your holy name.

> The meek shall eat and be satisfied: they shall praise the Lord that seek him: your heart shall live for ever.
>
> —Psalm 22:26

Lord, thank you for keeping us afloat in these difficult times. You give us what we need, and bestow your blessings on us. Let me be content and satisfied, and praise your name.

Grant us grace to see you, Lord,

Mirrored in your holy Word.

May our lives and all we do

Imitate and honor you

That we all like you may be

At your great epiphany

And may praise you, ever blest,

God in man made manifest.

—Christopher Wordsworth

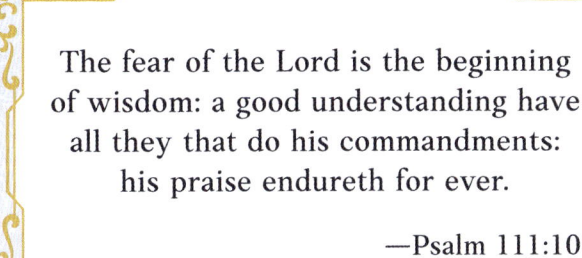

The fear of the Lord is the beginning of wisdom: a good understanding have all they that do his commandments: his praise endureth for ever.

—Psalm 111:10

You existed before the stars, Lord, and will exist after our own sun fails. How can I help but be in awe?

Enter into his gates with thanksgiving, and into his courts with praise: be thankful unto him, and bless his name.

—Psalm 100:4

All places belong to you, Lord. Whether I'm going to church on the weekend or walking through a glade of magnificent old trees in a forest preserve, let me praise your name.

> I thank thee, and praise thee, O thou God of my fathers, who hast given me wisdom and might, and hast made known unto me now what we desired of thee: for thou hast now made known unto us the king's matter.
>
> —Daniel 2:23

Lord, please give me a faith like the heroes of the Bible, who stood steadfast in their praise of you. Just as Daniel witnessed to King Nebuchadnezzar without fear or compromise, let me never be afraid to proclaim your name and works.

From the rising of the sun unto the going down of the same the Lord's name is to be praised.

—Psalm 113:3

It's easy to remember to praise God's name when I see a wonderful sunrise or sunset. Thank you, God, for natural beauty that reminds me to turn to you! Please also help me remember to praise your name when the sky is gray and dull.

> I will make thy name to be remembered in all generations: therefore shall the people praise thee for ever and ever.
>
> —Psalm 45:17

Lord, thank you for my godparents, an aunt and uncle who were always there for me. They took me out for dinner on my birthdays, made sure to talk with me at family parties, and kept in touch with me when I was in college. Through it all, they spoke of their own lives, and their strong faith too. They weren't heavy-handed about it, truly leading by example as they demonstrated their love and care in a way that mirrored God's love and care.

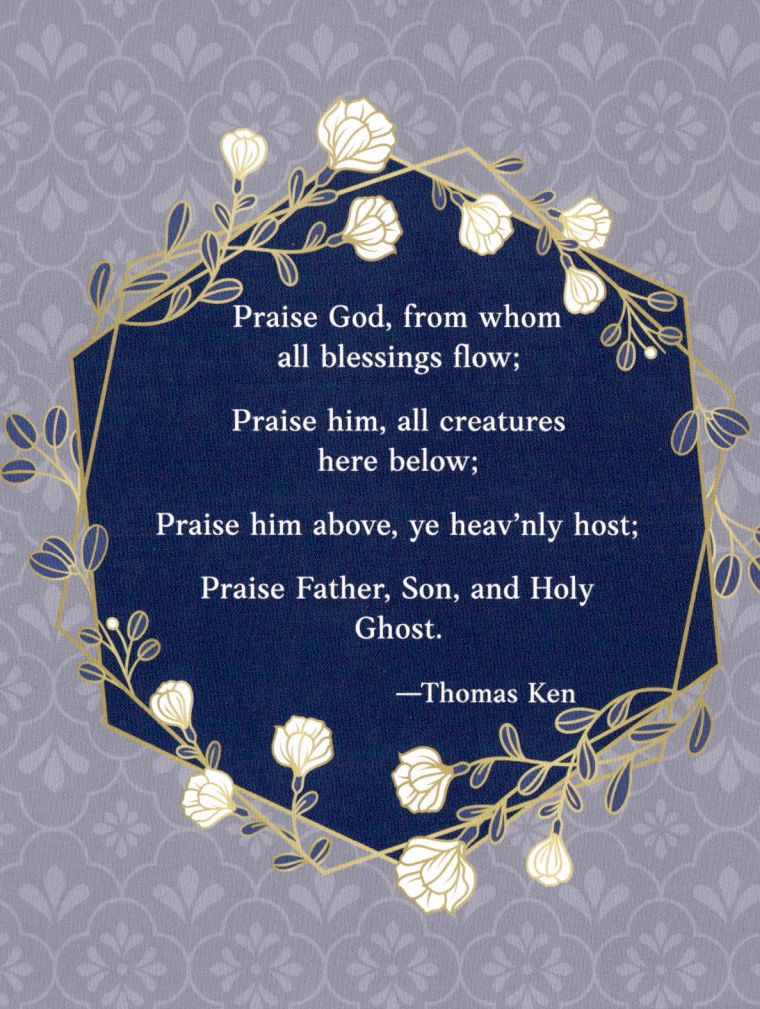

Praise God, from whom all blessings flow;

Praise him, all creatures here below;

Praise him above, ye heav'nly host;

Praise Father, Son, and Holy Ghost.

—Thomas Ken

> According to thy name, O God,
> so is thy praise unto the ends of
> the earth: thy right hand is full of
> righteousness.
>
> —Psalm 48:10

Occasionally when I pray alone at home, I'm reminded that though I may be alone physically, I'm not alone spiritually. Throughout Earth, other people are praying at the same time, and even if we don't know each other, we worship you together.

> And now shall mine head be lifted up above mine enemies round about me: therefore will I offer in his tabernacle sacrifices of joy; I will sing, yea, I will sing praises unto the Lord.
>
> —Psalm 27:6

I've wrapped up a big project at work, conquering my own fears, worries, and self-doubts. I'm holding my head high today, pleased with my accomplishment, and grateful for your help and guidance. Praise you, Jesus!

For the grave cannot praise thee, death can not celebrate thee: they that go down into the pit cannot hope for thy truth. The living, the living, he shall praise thee, as I do this day: the father to the children shall make known thy truth.

—Isaiah 38:18–19

Sometimes I push off prayer to "later"—off to the evening if it's a busy day, off to the weekend if it's a busy week. I think I'll have more time to spend in prayer or doing volunteer work when I'm retired or when the kids are grown. Please help me choose prayer and praise now, today, at this moment.

Thou art my God, and I will praise thee: thou art my God, I will exalt thee.

—Psalm 118:28

I bow down before you today, Lord, kneeling before you and raising my hands in prayer.

Praise him, praise him!

Jesus, our blessed redeemer!

Sing, O earth, his wonderful love proclaim!

Hail him, hail him!

Highest archangels in glory!

Strength and honor give to his holy name!

Like a shepherd, Jesus will guard his children.

In his arms he carries them all day long.

—Fanny Crosby

I will praise thee; for I am fearfully and wonderfully made: marvellous are thy works; and that my soul knoweth right well.

—Psalm 139:14

Thank you for this body, Lord. Thank you for these arms that can hug my husband and children, these hands that can put on bandages and braid hair, these feet that can carry me next door to check in on my elderly neighbor. Thank you for taste and touch and sight and sound, for eyelashes that protect my eyes and skin that heals when it's bruised. What a marvel the human body is.

Whoso offereth praise glorifieth me: and to him that ordereth his conversation aright will I shew the salvation of God.

—Psalm 50:23

Thank you, Lord, for this promise. I want to glorify and praise your name.

Rejoice in the Lord, O ye righteous: for praise is comely for the upright. Praise the Lord with harp: sing unto him with the psaltery and an instrument of ten strings. Sing unto him a new song; play skilfully with a loud noise. For the word of the Lord is right; and all his works are done in truth.

—Psalm 33:1–4

They started a new handbell choir at church, and it adds something to our worship. Thank you for those musicians and their instruments! How right it feels to praise you with song.

> And they sang together by course in praising and giving thanks unto the Lord; because he is good, for his mercy endureth for ever toward Israel. And all the people shouted with a great shout, when they praised the Lord, because the foundation of the house of the Lord was laid.
>
> —Ezra 3:11

We have no plans for a new church building, but a committee on which I serve did redecorate the interior for the season with flowers and banners. It felt good to give attention to the space where we worship, adding the little touches that help people settle into the space. For beauty and color, we praise you, alleluia!

Praise to the Lord,

The Almighty, the King of creation!

O my soul, praise him,

For he is your health and salvation!

Come, all who hear;

Now to his temple draw near,

Join me in glad adoration.

—Joachim Neander, trans. Catherine Winkworth

Thou hast turned for me my mourning into dancing: thou hast put off my sackcloth, and girded me with gladness; To the end that my glory may sing praise to thee, and not be silent. O Lord my God, I will give thanks unto thee for ever.

—Psalm 30:11–12

It's been two years since my sister's husband passed. Yesterday we met for the anniversary and shared memories, and it was a good day of healing. While my sister still grieves, she has a newfound peace and serenity in recent months. Thank you, Lord, for sustaining my sister through her grief and restoring joy to her life.

Praise ye the Lord. Praise ye the Lord from the heavens: praise him in the heights. Praise ye him, all his angels: praise ye him, all his hosts. Praise ye him, sun and moon: praise him, all ye stars of light. Praise him, ye heavens of heavens, and ye waters that be above the heavens. Let them praise the name of the Lord: for he commanded, and they were created. He hath also stablished them for ever and ever: he hath made a decree which shall not pass.

Praise the Lord from the earth, ye dragons, and all deeps: Fire, and hail; snow, and vapours; stormy wind fulfilling his word:

Mountains, and all hills; fruitful trees, and all cedars: Beasts, and all cattle; creeping things, and flying fowl:

Kings of the earth, and all people; princes, and all judges of the earth: Both young men, and maidens; old men, and children: Let them praise the name of the Lord: for his name alone is excellent; his glory is above the earth and heaven. He also exalteth the horn of his people, the praise of all his saints; even of the children of Israel, a people near unto him. Praise ye the Lord.

—Psalm 148

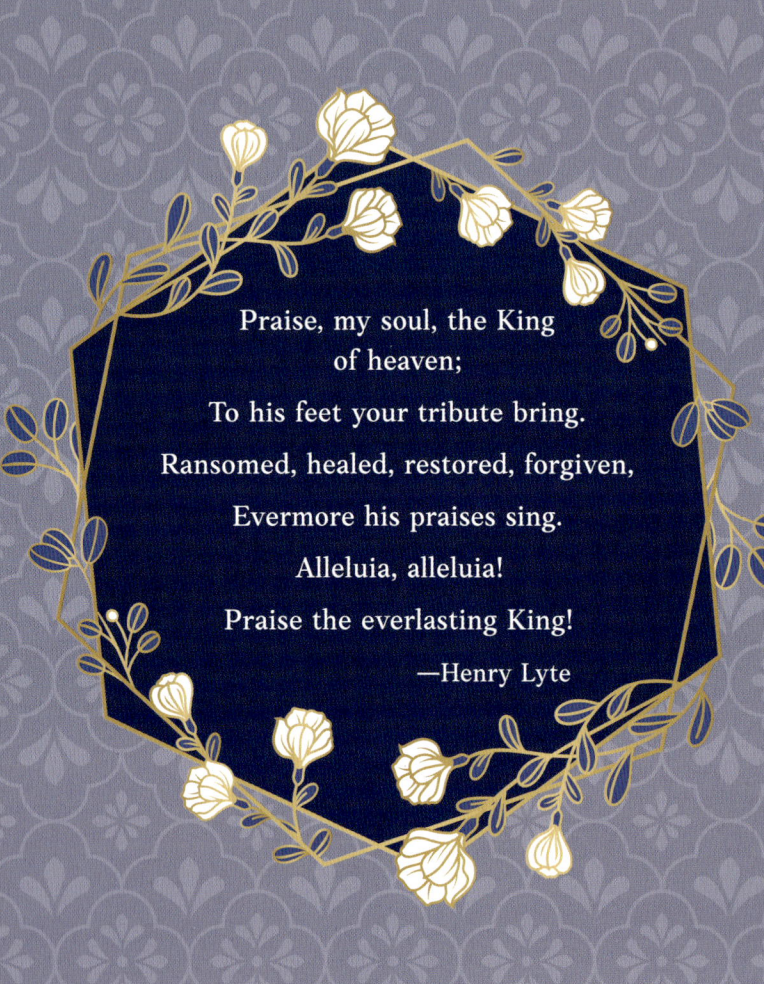

Praise, my soul, the King
of heaven;
To his feet your tribute bring.
Ransomed, healed, restored, forgiven,
Evermore his praises sing.
Alleluia, alleluia!
Praise the everlasting King!

—Henry Lyte

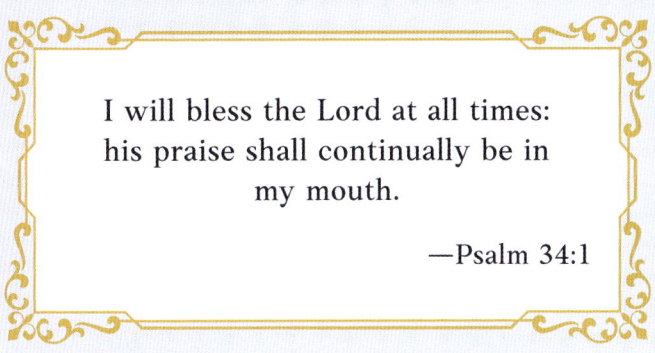

> I will bless the Lord at all times: his praise shall continually be in my mouth.
>
> —Psalm 34:1

When I look back over the day, often I realize how much I have to be grateful for and happy about. Lord, will you help me realize my blessings as I experience them? Let me remember to praise your name when I see a deer in the forest preserve on my morning commute, find the right words in a work meeting, watch my daughter's volleyball game, and appreciate the smells and tastes of dinner. Let me praise you in the moment, not just after the fact.

When the people rejoiced, for that they offered willingly, because with perfect heart they offered willingly to the Lord: and David the king also rejoiced with great joy. Wherefore David blessed the Lord before all the congregation: and David said, Blessed be thou, Lord God of Israel our father, for ever and ever. Thine, O Lord is the greatness, and the power, and the glory, and the victory, and the majesty: for all that is in the heaven and in the earth is thine; thine is the kingdom, O Lord, and thou art exalted as head above all. Both riches and honour come of thee, and thou reignest over all; and in thine hand is power and might; and in thine hand it is to make great, and to give strength unto all. Now therefore, our God, we thank thee, and praise thy glorious name.

—1 Chronicles 29:9–13

> Be thou exalted, O God, above the heavens; let thy glory be above all the earth. ... My heart is fixed, O God, my heart is fixed: I will sing and give praise. Awake up, my glory; awake, psaltery and harp: I myself will awake early. I will praise thee, O Lord, among the people: I will sing unto thee among the nations.
>
> —Psalm 57:5, 7–9

Let me begin my morning with praise, from the moment my feet hit the floor as I get out of bed!

> Who can utter the mighty acts of the Lord? who can shew forth all his praise?
>
> —Psalm 106:2

I don't know all your workings, Lord. I can't count the stars, nor do I know how many species of birds or bugs or fish there are. What I do see, I appreciate!

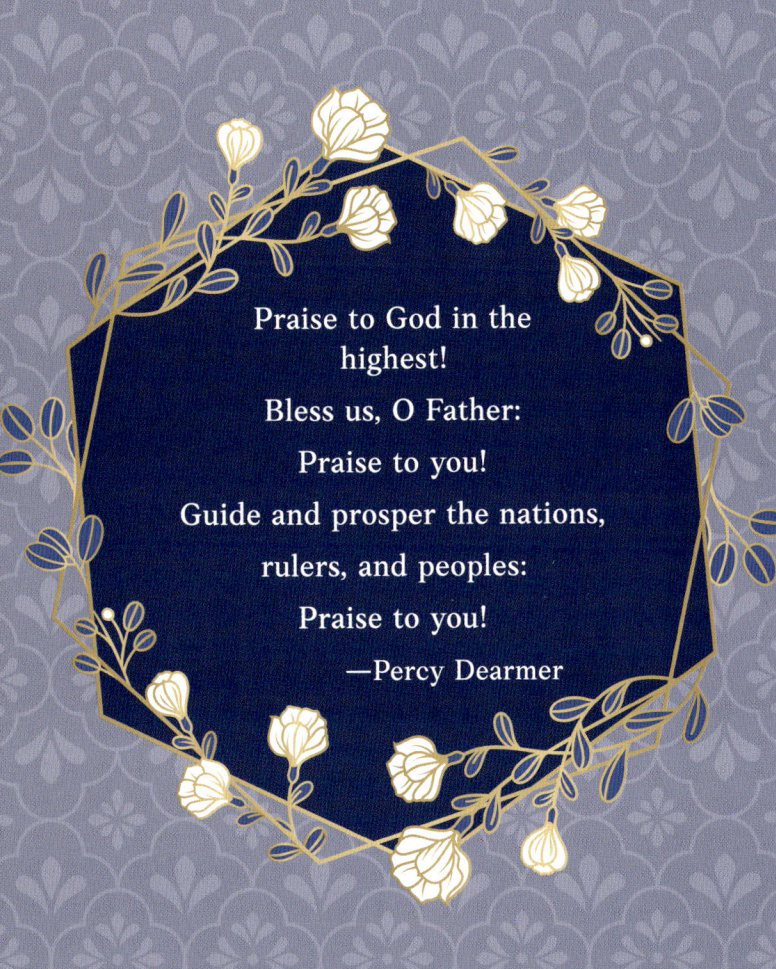

Praise to God in the highest!

Bless us, O Father:

Praise to you!

Guide and prosper the nations, rulers, and peoples:

Praise to you!

—Percy Dearmer

And my tongue shall speak of thy righteousness and of thy praise all the day long.

—Psalm 35:28

My youngest one is still at home, too young for school, and I am appreciating this time with her. In raising my daughter, in trying to teach her about you and offer prayers of praise and thanksgiving, I realize your goodness anew.

Sing unto the Lord a new song, and his praise from the end of the earth, ye that go down to the sea, and all that is therein; the isles, and the inhabitants thereof. Let the wilderness and the cities thereof lift up their voice, the villages that Kedar doth inhabit: let the inhabitants of the rock sing, let them shout from the top of the mountains. Let them give glory unto the Lord, and declare his praise in the islands.

—Isaiah 42:10–12

> Let the heaven and earth praise him, the seas, and every thing that moveth therein.
>
> —Psalm 69:34

We visited the zoo today. What a variety of creations you have made, God! We find peace and wonder in watching the giraffes amble about, admiring the snakes resting in the sun, and viewing the dolphins as they leap and swim. All your creations praise you!

We praise you, O God,

Our Redeemer, Creator;

In grateful devotion our tribute we bring;

We lay it before you;

We kneel and adore you;

We bless your holy name:

Glad praises we sing.

—Julia Cory

In God we boast all the day long, and praise thy name for ever.

—Psalm 44:8

How shall I praise your name today? What works of yours shall I boast about? I am grateful for all you do!

O Lord, how manifold are thy works! in wisdom hast thou made them all: the earth is full of thy riches. So is this great and wide sea, wherein are things creeping innumerable, both small and great beasts. There go the ships: there is that leviathan, whom thou hast made to play therein. These wait all upon thee; that thou mayest give them their meat in due season. That thou givest them they gather: thou openest thine hand, they are filled with good. Thou hidest thy face, they are troubled: thou takest away their breath, they die, and return to their dust. Thou sendest forth thy spirit, they are created: and thou renewest the face of the earth. The glory of the Lord shall endure for ever: the Lord shall rejoice in his works.

—Psalm 104:24–31

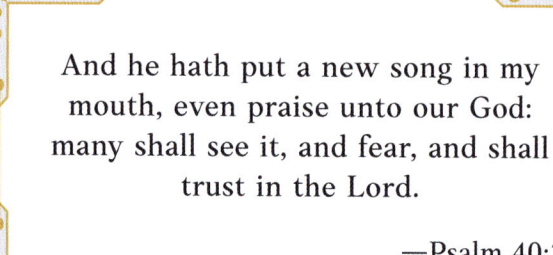

And he hath put a new song in my mouth, even praise unto our God: many shall see it, and fear, and shall trust in the Lord.

—Psalm 40:3

I've made a concerted effort in these last few months to stop grumbling and complaining. I don't want to be negative all the time! At first it required a lot of effort, but as time has gone on, I've found it much easier to think and say more positive things. Thank you, Lord, for putting a new song in my mouth!

Then will I go unto the altar of God, unto God my exceeding joy: yea, upon the harp will I praise thee, O God my God.

—Psalm 43:4

You are truly the source of my joy, Lord, and I lift my voice to praise you.

> O bless our God, ye people, and make the voice of his praise to be heard: Which holdeth our soul in life, and suffereth not our feet to be moved.
>
> —Psalm 66:8–9

So often, there's societal pressure to get ahead, to focus on building one's own wealth and status. Let me remember always to care for the poor, the widow, the orphan, as the Bible calls us to do. When I would falter and get distracted, keep my eyes on you, my mouth singing your praises, and my feet from being moved.

By thee have I been holden up
from the womb: thou art he that
took me out of my mother's bowels:
my praise shall be continually of thee.

—Psalm 71:6

Thank you for the gift of life, Lord.
You have cared for me since the very
beginning, and I thank you for it.

When I remember these things, I pour out my soul in me: for I had gone with the multitude, I went with them to the house of God, with the voice of joy and praise, with a multitude that kept holyday. Why art thou cast down, O my soul? and why art thou disquieted in me? hope thou in God: for I shall yet praise him for the help of his countenance.

—Psalm 42:4–5

Even when I'm discouraged, please help me remember to praise you. Let me make a habit of it, whether I'm in community or alone, happy or sad.

Thus will I bless thee while I live: I will lift up my hands in thy name. My soul shall be satisfied as with marrow and fatness; and my mouth shall praise thee with joyful lips.

—Psalm 63:4–5

Thank you so much for all your many gifts and blessings. I praise your holy name!

God be merciful unto us, and bless us; and cause his face to shine upon us; Selah.

That thy way may be known upon earth, thy saving health among all nations. Let the people praise thee, O God; let all the people praise thee. O let the nations be glad and sing for joy: for thou shalt judge the people righteously, and govern the nations upon earth. Selah.

Let the people praise thee, O God; let all the people praise thee. Then shall the earth yield her increase; and God, even our own God, shall bless us. God shall bless us; and all the ends of the earth shall fear him.

—Psalm 67

And a voice came out of the throne, saying, Praise our God, all ye his servants, and ye that fear him, both small and great. And I heard as it were the voice of a great multitude, and as the voice of many waters, and as the voice of mighty thunderings, saying, Alleluia: for the Lord God omnipotent reigneth.

—Revelation 19:5–6

THANKSGIVING

> Keep me as the apple of the eye, hide me under the shadow of thy wings.
>
> —Psalm 17:8

I remember when I was a young child, and the grandmotherly neighbor lit up with delight every time she saw me. How could I resist that joy? Lord, your delight in me is a gift, one that I don't deserve, but one that makes me want to spend time in your presence. Thank you for treating me as a treasure.

I thank God, whom I serve from my forefathers with pure conscience, that without ceasing I have remembrance of thee in my prayers night and day.

—2 Timothy 1:3

This prayer of Paul's was directed to Timothy, whom he called his "dearly beloved son." Today, I remember my own children, as well as those I've mentored or guided over the years. I thank you, God, for each of them, and pray for your blessings upon them.

Sing unto
the Lord with thanksgiving;
sing praise upon the harp unto
our God.

—Psalm 147:7

Thanks and praise so often go together in the Psalms. When I feel grateful, I want to praise your name, God of all!

> O give thanks unto the Lord; call upon his name: make known his deeds among the people.
>
> —Psalm 105:1

My husband is a man of deep faith, but it's often expressed through actions instead of words. Today he told me that he had almost been hit by another car during his ride to work, and he said spontaneously, "That could have been bad. Thank the Lord it wasn't!" Thank you, God, for the gift of my husband's safety, and for his impulse to make your deed known to me!

> So we thy people and sheep of thy pasture will give thee thanks for ever: we will shew forth thy praise to all generations.
>
> —Psalm 79:13

Lord, will you please help us instill in our children a deep and lasting faith? I want them to grow up knowing they are your people, part of a chain of faith that goes back generations.

Then they took away the stone from the place where the dead was laid. And Jesus lifted up his eyes, and said, Father, I thank thee that thou hast heard me. And I knew that thou hearest me always: but because of the people which stand by I said it, that they may believe that thou hast sent me.

—John 11:41–42

Jesus prayed, trusting that he was heard, before raising Lazarus from the dead. Please let me grow in faith, trusting that you hear me like you heard your son. I want to believe that you hear me always!

> O come, let us sing unto the Lord: let us make a joyful noise to the rock of our salvation. Let us come before his presence with thanksgiving, and make a joyful noise unto him with psalms. For the Lord is a great God, and a great King above all gods.
>
> —Psalm 95:1–3

Today I turned on the radio to a Christian station and sang along. Thanks for all those musicians who, like David and the psalmists of old, create songs of praise for us to raise our voices in worship!

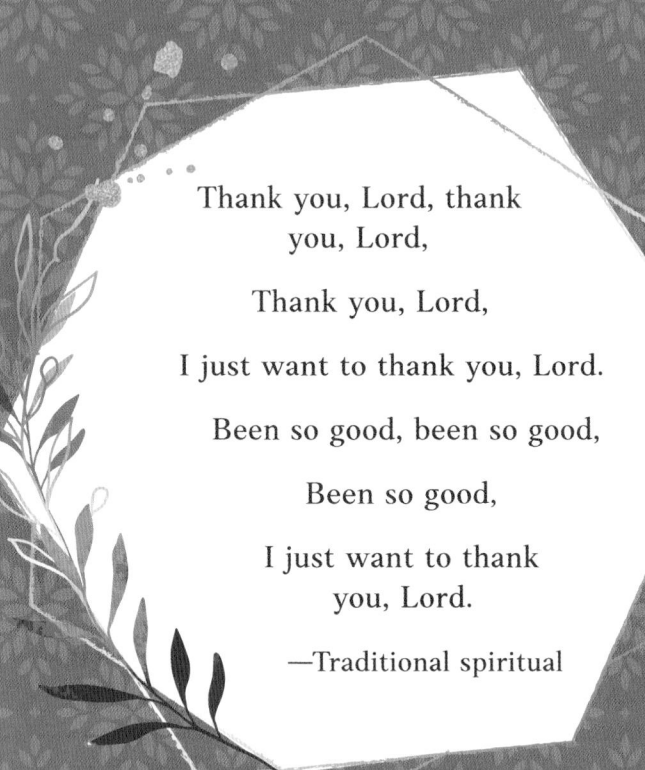

Thank you, Lord, thank you, Lord,

Thank you, Lord,

I just want to thank you, Lord.

Been so good, been so good,

Been so good,

I just want to thank you, Lord.

—Traditional spiritual

> But thanks be to God, which giveth us the victory through our Lord Jesus Christ.
>
> —1 Corinthians 15:57

A good friend recently transitioned to hospice care after a long battle with cancer. Though I'm grieving, I am comforted that she is at peace with her decision. Her strong faith is an example for me. Thank you, God, for your victory over sin and death, which means that we do not have to be afraid.

> Offer unto God thanksgiving; and pay thy vows unto the most High: And call upon me in the day of trouble: I will deliver thee, and thou shalt glorify me.
>
> —Psalm 50:14–15

You save me, Lord, again and again, delivering me from evil. Thank you!

Now thank we all our God

With heart and hands and voices,

Who wondrous things has done,

In whom his world rejoices;

Who from our mother's arms

Has blessed us on our way

With countless gifts of love,

And still is ours today.

—Martin Rinkart, trans. Catherine Winkworth

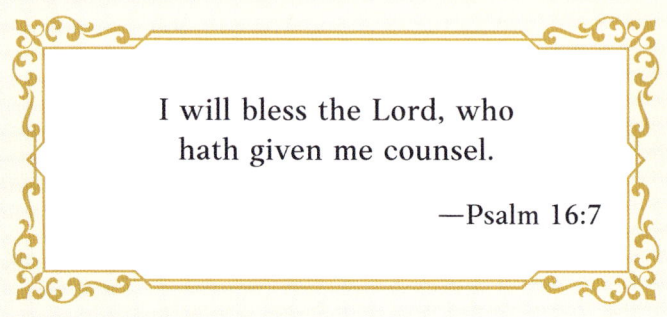

I will bless the Lord, who hath given me counsel.

—Psalm 16:7

We moved recently for my husband's job, and now that we've settled into our new home, I'm having to make some decisions. Do I continue to work remotely for my old job or look for something local? Which church should we attend? What activities should I get involved in? Lord, please give me counsel during this time, as you have in the past. Thank you in advance for your guidance.

Rejoice in the Lord, ye righteous; and give thanks at the remembrance of his holiness.

—Psalm 97:12

I don't feel righteous at the moment, or like rejoicing. But I do want to be righteous. I ask you to help me change my attitude, Father. I offer you thanks for your steadfast holiness.

> I will praise the name of God
> with a song, and will magnify him
> with thanksgiving.
>
> —Psalm 69:30

When my daughter was younger, she would sometimes burst into spontaneous songs about something that made her happy. I remember her singing one about a butterfly, "Pretty, pretty butterfly, you're so pretty, butterfly." May I have her same lack of self-consciousness and joy in singing spontaneous songs to you, Lord!

Rejoice, the Lord is King:

Your Lord and King adore!

Rejoice, give thanks and sing,

And triumph evermore.

Lift up your heart,

Lift up your voice!

Rejoice, again I say, rejoice!

—Charles Wesley

Thou hast also given me the shield of thy salvation: and thy right hand hath holden me up, and thy gentleness hath made me great.

—Psalm 18:35

This verse reminds me of my father. He was a strong, forthright man, but with his wife and daughters, he was very gentle and protective. On family walks, if we passed a house with a barking dog, he would stand between us and the dog, just in case. Thank you, my heavenly Father, for your love, protection, and gentleness.

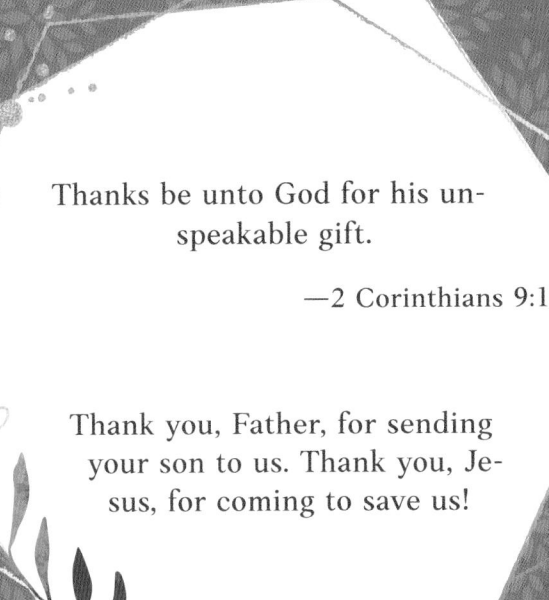

Thanks be unto God for his unspeakable gift.

—2 Corinthians 9:15

Thank you, Father, for sending your son to us. Thank you, Jesus, for coming to save us!

I will wash mine hands in innocency: so will I compass thine altar, O Lord: That I may publish with the voice of thanksgiving, and tell of all thy wondrous works.

—Psalm 26:6–7

Lord, thank you for the wonderful gift of forgiveness. When I confess my sins to you and accept your forgiveness, I feel much lighter and freer, able to focus on your awesome love and power instead of my own faults and flaws.

Rejoice, O pure in heart,

Rejoice, give thanks, and sing;

Your festal banner wave on high,

The cross of Christ your King.

Rejoice, rejoice, rejoice,

Give thanks, and sing!

—Edward Plumptre

> Unto thee, O God, do we give thanks, unto thee do we give thanks: for that thy name is near thy wondrous works declare.
>
> —Psalm 75:1

We've started a new project in our Bible study: each day for one month, we'll share via e-mail one thing for which we're grateful. We're only a week in, but I love it! On days when I wake up on the wrong side of the bed, seeing those e-mails lifts my heart. A grateful heart is a happy one!

My God, I thank thee, who hast made

The earth so bright;

So full of splendor and of joy,

Beauty and light,

So many glorious things are here,

Noble and right.

—Adelaide Procter

> The heaven, even the heavens, are the Lord's: but the earth hath he given to the children of men.
>
> —Psalm 115:16

Thank you, Lord, for mountains and plains, oceans and deserts, fields full of crops and orchards full of fruit trees. Thank you for the beauty of shells and rocks, butterflies and birds, flowers and trees. Thank you for the beauty of this wonderful world!

> Praise ye the Lord. O give thanks unto the Lord; for he is good: for his mercy endureth for ever.
>
> —Psalm 106:1

Well, I've screwed up, Lord. You'd think I'd have learned by now how to avoid losing my temper, but here we are again. Thank you, though, for your enduring mercy—I need it!

Give thanks unto God and
be joyful,

Whatever may daily befall,

Rejoice in the Lord,
thy Redeemer,

Who ruleth supreme over all.

—Julia Johnston

> At midnight I will rise to give thanks unto thee because of thy righteous judgments.
>
> —Psalm 119:62

I haven't been sleeping well, with too many worries on my mind. I'm trying to redirect my mind when I wake up. Instead of dwelling on my worries, I give thanks for my blessings. The insomnia persists, but I've found that I don't mind quite as much, when I'm spending my time awake focusing on gratitude rather than distress!

Praise ye the Lord!

Give thanks and sing;

Tell of his love to ev'ry land
and nation,

Praise ye the Lord,

Give thanks and sing,

Praise him forever,

Who bringeth salvation.

—Eliza Hewitt

Let the heavens rejoice, and let the earth be glad; let the sea roar, and the fulness thereof. Let the field be joyful, and all that is therein: then shall all the trees of the wood rejoice.

—Psalm 96:11–12

Thank you, God, for nature! Even a walk around the neighborhood can lift my mood, and there's nothing like a longer hike on the weekend, when I'm surrounded by the sounds of nature. Thank you for those times of joy.

In that hour Jesus rejoiced in spirit, and said, I thank thee, O Father, Lord of heaven and earth, that thou hast hid these things from the wise and prudent, and hast revealed them unto babes: even so, Father; for so it seemed good in thy sight.

—Luke 10:21

Lord, please give me the simple faith of a child. When I feel inadequate, thank you for the reminder that I don't need to be a genius or a learned theologian for you to love me!

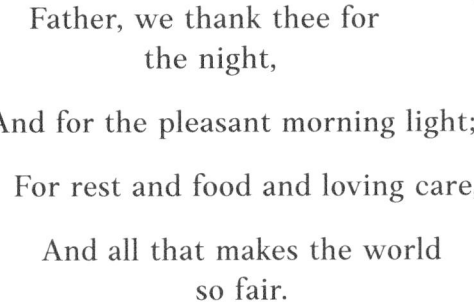

Father, we thank thee for the night,

And for the pleasant morning light;

For rest and food and loving care,

And all that makes the world so fair.

—Rebecca Weston

Oh that men would praise the Lord for his goodness, and for his wonderful works to the children of men! And let them sacrifice the sacrifices of thanksgiving, and declare his works with rejoicing.

—Psalm 107:21–22

Thank you, Lord, for your gifts to humanity. Thank you for making us able to love, think, dance, pray, and discover. Thank you for curiosity and ingenuity and, above all, wisdom.

It is a good thing to give thanks unto the Lord, and to sing praises unto thy name, O Most High: To shew forth thy lovingkindness in the morning, and thy faithfulness every night, Upon an instrument of ten strings, and upon the psaltery; upon the harp with a solemn sound.

—Psalm 92:1–3

Surely the righteous shall
give thanks unto thy name: the
upright shall dwell in
thy presence.

—Psalm 140:13

I want to dwell in your presence,
God. I want a deeper relationship with you. I want to
follow you more closely.

> I will offer to thee the sacrifice
> of thanksgiving, and will call upon the
> name of the Lord.
>
> —Psalm 116:17

I thank you, God, every day and every hour. I thank you for my family and friends. I thank you for my work and my hobbies. Most of all, I thank you for your presence in my life!

Give thanks to God,
for good is he:

His love abides forever.

To him all praise and glory be:

His mercy lasts forever.

His wondrous works with
praise record:

His love abides forever.

The only God, the sovereign
Lord:

His mercy lasts forever.

—Arthur Sullivan

> We give thee thanks, O Lord God Almighty, which art, and wast, and art to come; because thou hast taken to thee thy great power, and hast reigned.
>
> —Revelation 11:17

My mind boggles when I really try to think about your greatness and majesty. You know more than the greatest supercomputer. You have more power than the worst tyrant. Yet you are not distant or uncaring; You see my heart and my smallest concerns. Thank you!

It came even to pass, as the trumpeters and singers were as one, to make one sound to be heard in praising and thanking the Lord; and when they lifted up their voice with the trumpets and cymbals and instruments of musick, and praised the Lord, saying, For he is good; for his mercy endureth for ever: that then the house was filled with a cloud, even the house of the Lord; So that the priests could not stand to minister by reason of the cloud: for the glory of the Lord had filled the house of God.

—2 Chronicles 5:13–14

> And he took the seven loaves and the fishes, and gave thanks, and brake them, and gave to his disciples, and the disciples to the multitude.
>
> —Matthew 15:36

Thank you, Lord, for our family meals. Like Jesus, we offer thanks first, before we pass the dishes around to share our food. You are in our midst, as we laugh and talk and share stories of our day. Thank you, Lord, for this common, everyday miracle.

GOD'S PRESENCE

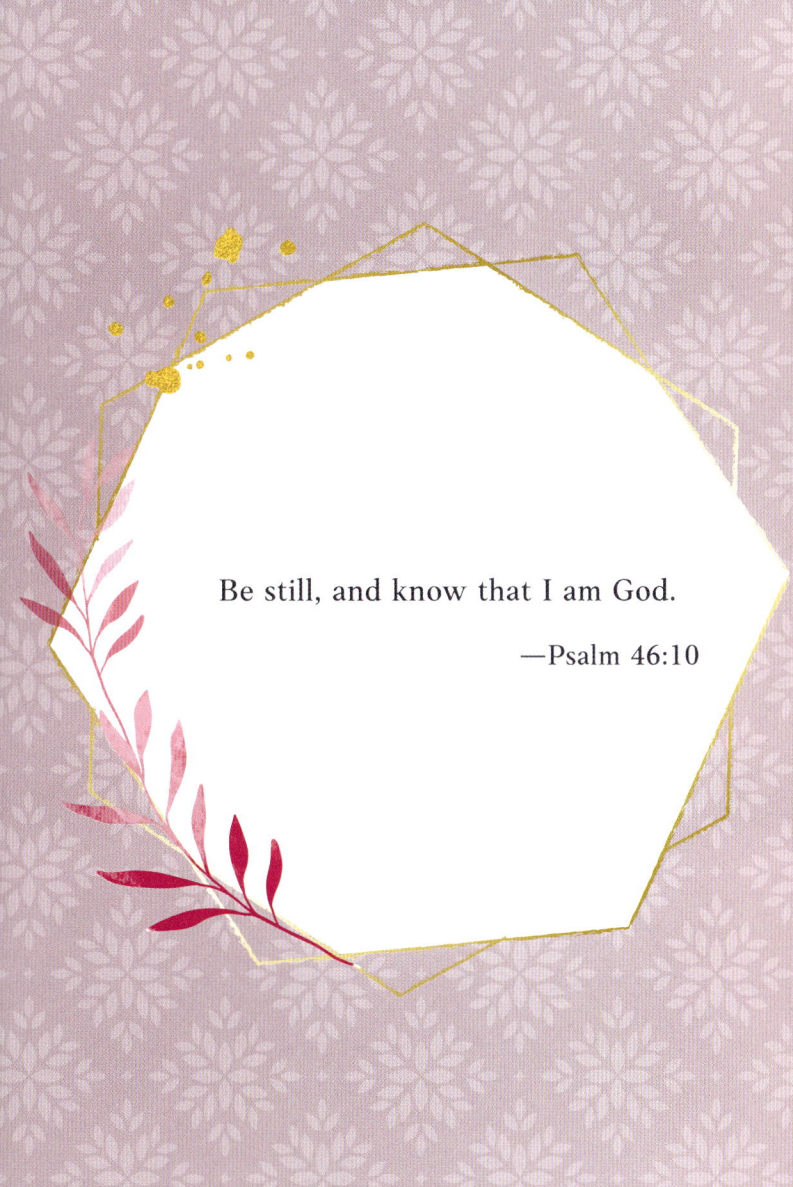

Be still, and know that I am God.

—Psalm 46:10

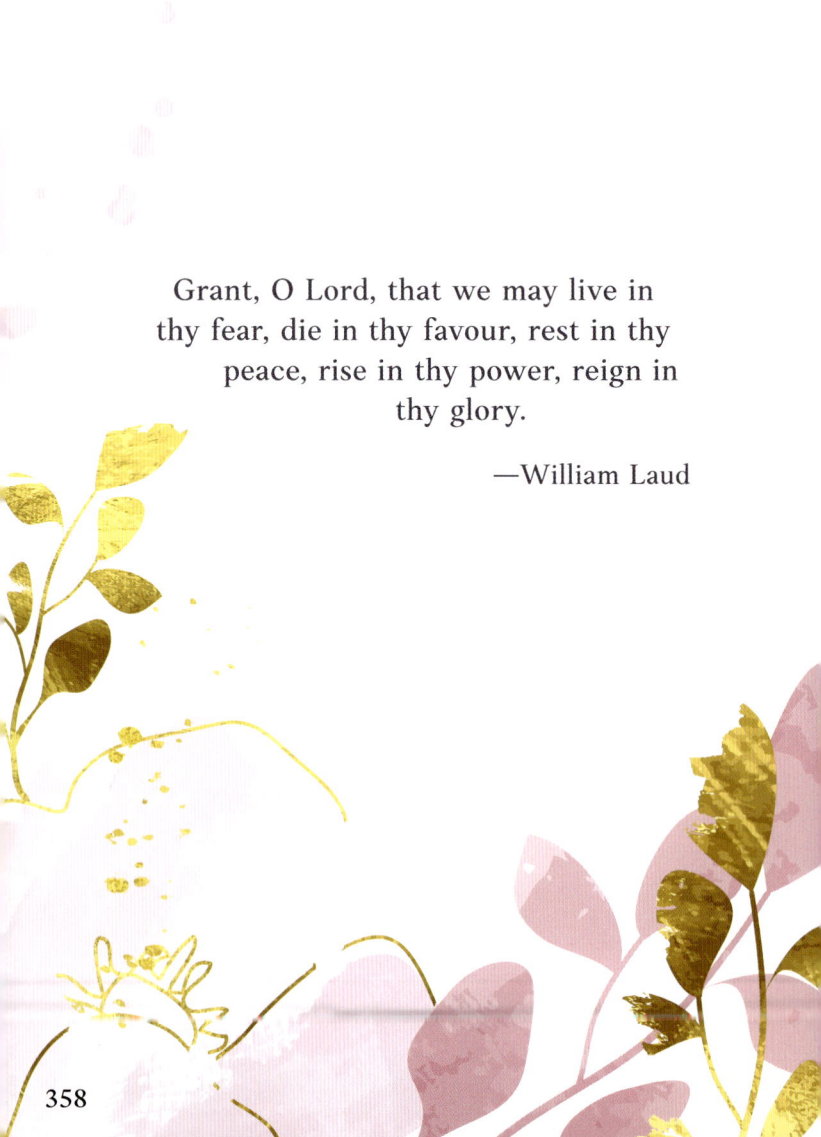

Grant, O Lord, that we may live in thy fear, die in thy favour, rest in thy peace, rise in thy power, reign in thy glory.

—William Laud

Thou wilt shew me the path of life: in thy presence is fulness of joy; at thy right hand there are pleasures for evermore.

—Psalm 16:11

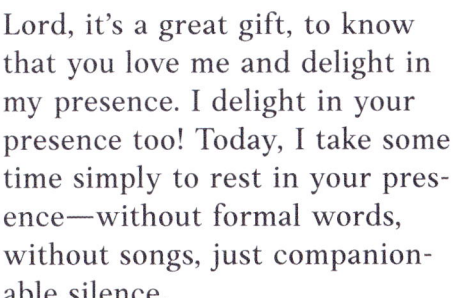

Lord, it's a great gift, to know that you love me and delight in my presence. I delight in your presence too! Today, I take some time simply to rest in your presence—without formal words, without songs, just companionable silence.

O most
   merciful Lord,
 grant to me thy grace,
  that it may be with me, and labour with me, and persevere with me even to the end. Grant that I may always desire and will that which is to thee most acceptable, and most dear. Let thy will be mine, and my will ever follow thine, and agree perfectly with it. Grant to me above all things that can be desired, to rest in thee, and in thee to have my heart at peace.

—Thomas à Kempis

Blessed is the man whom thou choosest, and causest to approach unto thee, that he may dwell in thy courts: we shall be satisfied with the goodness of thy house, even of thy holy temple.

—Psalm 65:4

Sometimes going to church or sitting down to pray feels like an obligation, but really it's an invitation to spend time with a loved one. Thank you for blessing me with the gift of faith, which makes me want to get closer to you.

Be the eye of God dwelling
with you

The foot of Christ in guidance
with you

The shower of the Spirit pouring
on you

Richly and generously.

—Alexander Carmichael

Whither shall I go from thy spirit? or whither shall I flee from thy presence? If I ascend up into heaven, thou art there: if I make my bed in hell, behold, thou art there. If I take the wings of the morning, and dwell in the uttermost parts of the sea; Even there shall thy hand lead me, and thy right hand shall hold me.

—Psalm 139:7–10

Sometimes I want to hide from you, God, especially when I've done something wrong and I feel guilty. Other times, it is a relief to be known and loved. You will never abandon me.

God's might to direct me.

God's power to protect me.

God's wisdom for my learning.

God's eye for my discerning.

God's ear for my hearing.

God's word for my clearing.

—St. Patrick

> For a day in thy courts is better than a thousand. I had rather be a doorkeeper in the house of my God, than to dwell in the tents of wickedness.
>
> —Psalm 84:10

God, I want my biggest goal to be seeking closeness with you. When I get distracted or place other desires above my desire to grow in faith and love, please gently guide me back to the right path.

I come to the garden alone,

While the dew is still on the roses;

And the voice I hear, falling on my ear,

The Son of God discloses.

And he walks with me, and he talks with me,

And he tells me I am his own,

And the joy we share as we tarry there,

None other has ever known.

—C. Austin Miles

> Glory ye in his holy name: let the heart of them rejoice that seek the Lord.
>
> —Psalm 105:3

Please draw me deeper into communion with you, Jesus. Let me seek your presence and revere your holy name.

> O God, thou art my God; early will I seek thee: my soul thirsteth for thee, my flesh longeth for thee in a dry and thirsty land, where no water is.
>
> —Psalm 63:1

It can be uncomfortable to seek, to yearn, to thirst. When I am uncomfortable and dissatisfied with my life, that's usually a sign that I'm missing you—that I haven't been spending enough time in prayer, or that my prayers have all been on the surface level. Where I seek other things to satisfy myself, please guide me back to your presence.

Serve the Lord with gladness: come before his presence with singing.

—Psalm 100:2

I can't say I ordinarily pray during my morning commute, unless I pray for help in case of an imminent accident, but today seemed like a good day to turn the radio to the Christian station and sing along. It was great to spend extra time with you, God!

They who seek the throne
of grace

Find that throne in every place;

If we live a life of prayer,

God is present everywhere.

—Oliver Holden

> When thou saidst, Seek ye my face; my heart said unto thee, Thy face, Lord, will I seek.
>
> —Psalm 27:8

My head can get tangled up in worries and guilt, but my heart knows that I want to be close to you. Thank you, God of love, for the heart's wisdom.

I will lift up mine eyes unto the hills, from whence cometh my help. My help cometh from the Lord, which made heaven and earth.

—Psalm 121:1–2

Life's been busy, God. I've been doing things that I think will please you: volunteer work and leading a small group in Bible study. Yet I've been feeling distant from you lately, and I think that means it's time to get out in nature this weekend to go hiking. On the trails, and at the overlook where I can see down into the valley below, I always feel your presence very strongly.

Be still, my soul!

The Lord is on your side;

Bear patiently the cross of grief
or pain;

Leave to your God to order
and provide;

In ev'ry change he faithful will remain.

Be still, my soul!

Your best, your heav'nly friend

Thru' thorny ways leads to a joyful end.

—Kathrina von Schlegel, trans. Jane Borthwick

> The earth shook, the heavens also dropped at the presence of God: even Sinai itself was moved at the presence of God, the God of Israel.
>
> —Psalm 68:8

The winds are picking up in advance of the storm that's forecast for tonight. Sometimes I see your power in the gentle beauty of a burbling stream. Tonight I'll see and hear it in lightning and thunder and roaring winds. Your power is awe-inspiring, Lord!

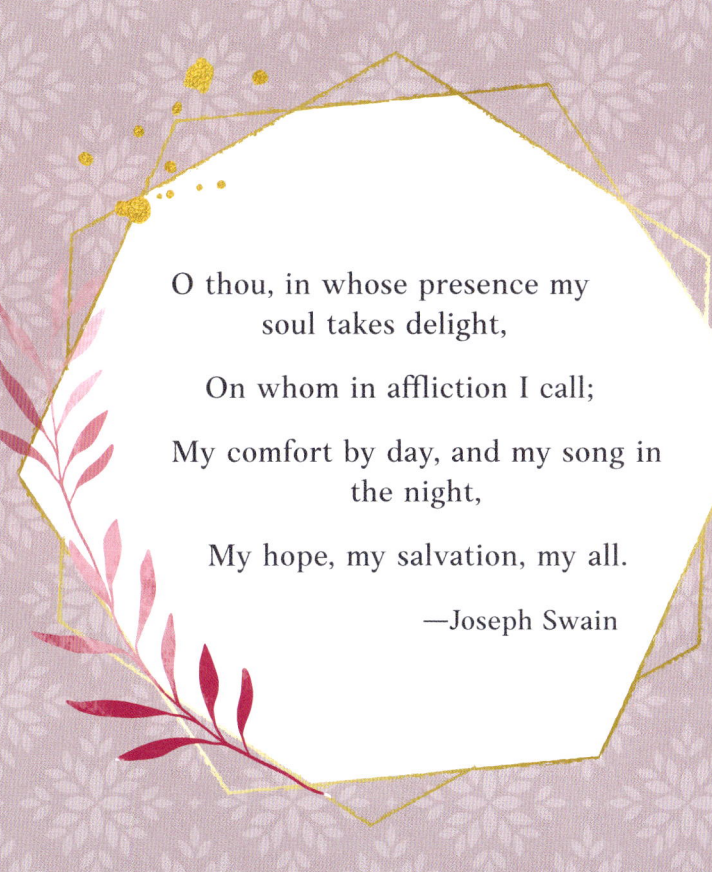

O thou, in whose presence my soul takes delight,

On whom in affliction I call;

My comfort by day, and my song in the night,

My hope, my salvation, my all.

—Joseph Swain

> As the hart panteth after the water brooks, so panteth my soul after thee, O God. My soul thirsteth for God, for the living God: when shall I come and appear before God?
>
> —Psalm 42:1–2

After a chaotic morning, the kids are off at school. Before I head out to work, I'm taking a moment just to be with you, Lord, to sit in silence and read your Word.

Thou shalt increase my greatness, and comfort me on every side.

—Psalm 71:21

Like Solomon, I ask for greatness in the form of wisdom: the wisdom to follow you, the wisdom to teach my children, and the wisdom to share my love for you with my friends.

Lord, in thy presence here we meet,

May we in thee be found;

O, make the place divinely sweet,

And let thy grace abound.

—J. L. Holman

> I was glad when they said unto me, Let us go into the house of the Lord.
>
> —Psalm 122:1

Whether I'm going to church or going to a friend's home for a prayer session or returning home after work to sing praise songs as I make dinner, let me be excited and glad to spend time with you.

God himself is present;

Let us now adore him

And with awe appear before him.

God is in his temple;

All within keep silence;

Humbly kneel in deepest rev'rence.

He alone

On his throne

Is our God and Savior;

Praise his name forever!

—Gerhardt Tersteegen, trans. John Miller and Frederick Foster

Mark the perfect man, and behold the upright: for the end of that man is peace.

—Psalm 37:37

Only with you, Lord, do I find true peace. Thank you for the peace of mind and heart that only you can provide, that I experience when I rest in your presence.

The righteous shall flourish like the palm tree: he shall grow like a cedar in Lebanon.

—Psalm 92:12

Lord, draw me to your Word! Give me a thirst for righteousness. I want to grow and flourish according to your ways, seeking your path instead of following my own. I want to choose to walk with you.

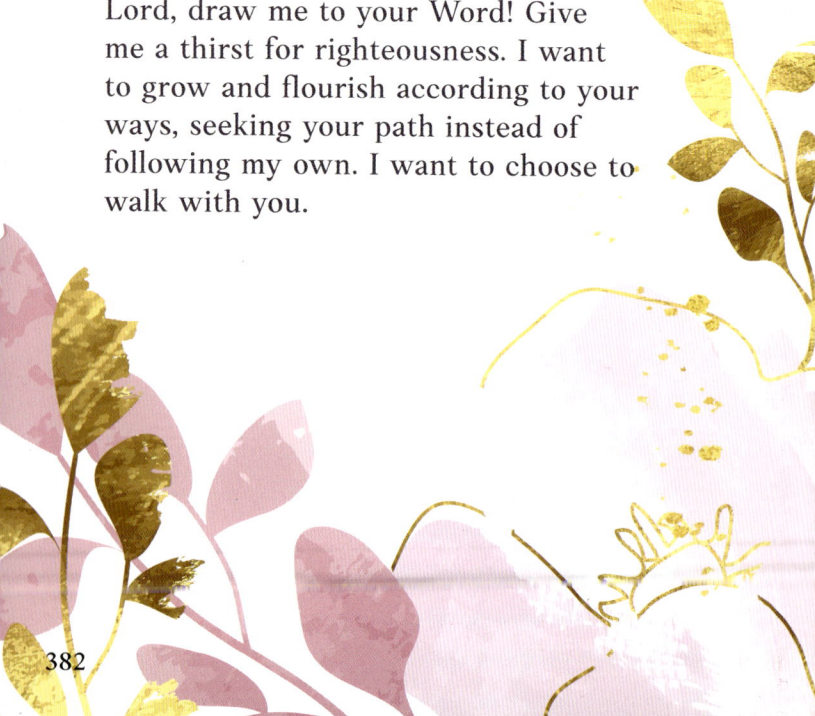

> One thing have I desired of the Lord, that will I seek after; that I may dwell in the house of the Lord all the days of my life, to behold the beauty of the Lord, and to enquire in his temple.
>
> —Psalm 27:4

This psalm reminds me of the story of Mary and Martha. Like Martha, I'm often busy doing things. But part of my soul wants, like Mary, simply to sit and listen at your feet, doing the "one thing [that] is needful" (Luke 10:42). When I'm distracted, Lord, help me focus on you.

Blessed is the man that walketh not in the counsel of the ungodly, nor standeth in the way of sinners, nor sitteth in the seat of the scornful. But his delight is in the law of the Lord; and in his law doth he meditate day and night. And he shall be like a tree planted by the rivers of water, that bringeth forth his fruit in his season; his leaf also shall not wither; and whatsoever he doeth shall prosper.

—Psalm 1:1–3